FROM BADLANDS TO BALI

ADVENTURES OF A TWENTIETH CENTURIY AMERICAN WANDERER

A MEMOIR

BY JEAN AHLNESS STEBINGER

BORN 1922

FROM BADLANDS TO BALI

MY ABC'S: ARROWHEADS, BADLANDS AND CATTLE

The dinky town in which I spent my early years was Rhame, North Dakota. It was one of the settlements founded by Norwegians and Swedes who ventured into Montana and the Dakotas in the first part of the twentieth century. What Europe lacked in those days, I don't know, but it is hard to believe the Dakota Territory was much better.

What did those early adventurers see around them? Certainly no trees or greenery. Instead there were miles and miles of buttes and badlands—not very inviting, perhaps, but beautiful in their way. The town of Rhame nestled in its own little valley, with buttes on either side rising up a couple hundred feet, leaving room for a village consisting of just four blocks in each direction and a population of only 300 people at its peak in 1930.

The land around town wasn't fertile enough for normal, crop-growing farms. Instead there were dry miles of prairie. The other primary feature was the badlands, which were mostly hills consisting of layers of rocks and clay, with prairie grasses between them. That may not sound very inviting, but it was lovely in its own fashion.

Also, though not much good for crops, the prairie grass made food for cattle and sheep. The dryness of the atmosphere, along with stingy rainfall, however, meant that a sizeable amount of land was required for each animal. No ranch could get by with less than 4000 acres, and more was better.

Obviously, people were sparse, and life was far from easy, but what a place for kids! Caves contained ancient petroglyphs, cliff sides were painted with bison, which had been considered holy by the native Indians, and large white stone circles indicated one-time teepee rings. Combined with that, thousands of hand-chipped stone arrowheads lay on or near the surface. It was a young explorer's dream world.

As to the town itself, Main Street was lined by two blocks of stores, including my pharmacist father's "Ahlness Drug Store." Since there were rarely any doctors living near, and the nearest hospital was 120 miles away in Montana, he did it all—setting bones, sewing up cuts, mixing medicines, or ordering them from Minneapolis, Minnesota 600 miles away. His clientele consisted of horses as well as humans.

Since I worked in the drug store during both my high school and college years, I had plenty of practice in my own way. When needed, for instance, I could manage to get a huge pill into a horse's throat by shoving into it a piece of hose, followed by a good-sized brass rod. Dad's job was to hang onto, and soothe, the horse.

The drug store also became a gathering place for youngsters and adults alike, so it was a pretty sociable place. Sometimes, though, I wondered how, with such limited skills, I would ever be able to earn a living in the larger world. Never mind, it was a wonderful way to grow up.

My youthful days were also a lesson in survival. The 1930's held not only a major Depression, but also days and days of what was called a "dust bowl." Crops, under those circumstances, grew very sparsely. For some folks, even starvation was never far away.

I give my parents a lot of credit for holding the community together. Dad would bring medicine to both town folks and ranchers whether they could pay for it or not, and later, when I looked over his books, I realized that, in a pinch, he even gave them cash. As for my mother, since such an extravagance as driving to the nearest town with a movie theater was out of the question, she simply taught everyone in Rhame to play cards—bridge and pinochle primarily. Soon card games played such a role that even the church's Ladies Aid Society, after a brief business meeting, brought out the decks!

It may seem to you like a dreary period and place for a childhood, but would I change mine? Definitely not.

The year I was five years old, Davy, the boy next door, and I spent much of our time climbing the trees my father had planted on the lawn around our house. Those leafy beauties were something of a miracle

4

themselves. Practically nothing but prairie grass would grow on the western North Dakota plains, so our trees were the only ones in town, and had taken infinite patience and exertion on Dad's part. Each tree required endless pails of water hauled up from our cistern and carefully poured over its roots a couple of times a day over a period of years.

That spring Davy waved a book at me with pictures of kids in Vermont (wherever that was) filling pails with maple syrup from trees. Why not do the same ourselves?

Carefully we formed our plan. Punching holes in a tree might cause syrup to spurt out, so we would start with that. If that wasn't enough we could carve out bigger pieces of bark. Not wasting a minute, we gathered pails and hammers, and then sneaked the heaviest knives we could find from our mothers' kitchens.

Armed and ready, we attacked the bark of the largest tree. It was smooth, all right, but turned out to be extremely thick and tough. Our 5-year-old muscles couldn't dent it. Giving up on holes, we changed our strategy. It took a couple of hours of slow and intense cutting before we managed to make a couple of long gashes in the surface. More hours were needed to peel back the thick bark from the trunk as we gradually managed to bare a couple of feet of its inside layer.

Tensely we peered to spot that yummy stuff underneath the bark, but no luck. Not a drop of maple syrup appeared—just a thin, sticky film with a sour taste. Unfortunately, Dad's trees were not maples. The picture book had betrayed us.

When my father came home that evening he nearly went into shock.

"You've killed my poplar!" he mourned over his precious once-sturdy specimen.

"Oh, so it's a poplar tree," Davy hissed to me. "How were *we* supposed to know?"

Davy's father came to help as the men tenderly patted the jagged strip, which extended nearly a quarter of the way around the tree's skin, back into place. Davy and I had managed to pull down a good-sized hunk. Chagrined, we rubbed our sore muscles, no longer proud of our prowess.

Well, the tree did survive, but the two of us nearly didn't. For years we were known as kids so dumb we would try to make maple syrup out of a poplar tree in North Dakota. Indeed, to this day no one has managed to succeed.

In the parched state of North Dakota during my childhood there was one very special day—June 15th. That spot on the calendar had been declared, of all things, the opening of fishing season. Frankly, considering the few spots where water collected at all, fish dinners rarely appeared on any tables. Still, it somehow continued to make a favorite men's hobby.

As an example, my father and other avid fishermen, determined not to waste a minute, could invariably be found at midnight each June 14th on the only water available at all—dammed up Coyote Creek, the sole spot to fish within fifty square miles. They brought their rowboats and fishing lines and I, in what was the best money-making opportunity of the year, provided worms. I sold them to the men for a nickel apiece, determined to amass enough to get that most prized of possessions, a bike.

Having spent most of my spare time during the spring identifying worm locations in our tiny town on the prairie, I was the fishermen's primary worm source. It was a pretty lucrative monopoly, in my opinion, and my pile of nickels grew.

Then, one day, near the pond, came my nemesis: a snapping turtle. As you can imagine, those large, nasty animals were a dangerous foe for a 10-year-old. I didn't dare chase them with a hoe to chop off their heads, since when I got close enough the turtle could bite me before I could even get my weapon in the air. A gun would have worked, but guns were forbidden for minors, except for the ones who snuck out with their fathers during hunting season.

Hunting season! That was my savior. It brought lots of enthusiastic men and their guns from states far to the South, each determined to take a bunch of pheasants back with them. To tell the truth, they downed many more grouse than pheasants, but never mind, they were all my friends. Since they found snapping turtles no more pleasant than I did, they simply shot the animals' heads off. Then, once again boss of my own territory, I could go back to worm-digging.

COULD WE MAKE A LIVING KILLING RATTLESNAKES?

My best friend at the age of eleven was Ethel, whose father was a rancher. Our favorite occupation during my frequent visits with her family was exploring, on horseback, other ranches that had been abandoned.

"That barn is sagging badly, and the family has been gone only a couple of years," one of us might observe pompously.

"And look at that rusty combine," the other would point out, determined to be equally profound. "How can machines rust so much when it never rains on them?"

There was always plenty to explore: houses, barns, machine sheds, chicken roosts, etc. Numerous pieces of forsaken farm machinery were also there to clamber over, and often fall off. We especially liked the house cellars, which were just the spot for lunch breaks on hot summer days.

Those cellars often had a space for a furnace dug out from the dirt, but little room beyond that. They were lit by windows at ground level set back a little from the room itself. That left a ledge, usually a couple of feet wide, all around the room. The cool dampness of a dirt cellar, dim light filtering through its cob-webbed windows, was welcome respite on a sweltering August day. There we unwrapped our sandwiches with pleasure.

One day, in a darker-than-usual basement, I saw movement beside me on the ledge and put out my hand.

"Yeow!" I yelled. "It's a snake!"

The snake was a large one, also enjoying the cool place. It slithered away at my touch but of course ruined our peaceful lunch.

When we related the story afterward, Ethel's older brother, Norman, whom we considered the source of all wisdom, declared it was probably a black snake.

"You girls should have been glad for its company," he averred. "Black snakes aren't poisonous and wouldn't bother you. Also, they kill rattlesnakes, which might. Rattlesnakes kill our chickens, too, so we definitely don't want them around the ranch."

The next time we went out wandering, what should we spot on our way home but a rattlesnake. It was in a field only a couple of miles from the house.

"Let's kill it," determined Ethel.

"But how?" I wanted to know.

"Rocks," she insisted, so we jumped off our horses and picked up some large stones that were lying near the trail. Each of us threw the biggest rocks we could find, but the snake seemed totally disinterested, probably because we generally missed.

"We need bigger rocks," I decided. "There are some on that small butte behind us. You stay and watch the snake and the horses while I run and get an armful."

Buttes, those eroded hills called badlands, always had plenty of rocks on top. I dashed up and returned with as many as I could carry. It didn't take us long to heave them at our target.

This time we got more reaction. The rattler receded to a small bush and wound itself into a coil, head sticking out the top and facing our direction, its tongue flicking occasionally.

"Now it's my turn to get rocks," offered Ethel, whereupon she brought back another small pile.

"They'll be really proud of us for killing a rattlesnake," I announced grandly. "We can start killing them every time we see one, and make quite a reputation for ourselves."

9

Ethel agreed. Taking careful aim at the snake's head, we threw our new rocks with all our strength. When we had heaved them all, we and the snake were still at an impasse. After a couple more turns at bringing additional ammunition, we were tired of running to and from the butte. By this time the creature was surrounded by our stones, but didn't look any the worse from our efforts.

"You stay on this side where he can watch you," I plotted. "I'll go around behind him and pick up rocks."

I promptly did so, managing to recoup several good-sized ones. These we threw in turn. By that time we must have been at our project for at least an hour.

About then we heard a truck. It was Norman, sent to find us.

"Here you are," he called. "You're late for lunch—what the heck is keeping you?"

Then he spotted the coiled rattlesnake.

"Are you kids crazy?" he bawled. "That snake is curled up and ready to strike! Get on home."

Chagrined, we got on our horses and headed for the ranch house.

At lunch, Norman said he had shot the rattler.

"I'll go back to the same place tomorrow and kill its mate," he commented. "The mate always stays around a while. I can probably just chop that one's head off with a hoe."

"Those girls are lucky," the family agreed. We hung our heads, which were no longer filled with dreams of glory.

From then on, Ethel and I stuck to observing deserted buildings and moldering machines. And riding harmless horses.

COLLEGE ON A SHOESTRING PLUS POKER DICE

If you think surviving the depression in North Dakota was perilous, you should have tried paying for two daughters in college even when the depression seemed to be over. The former turned out to be just a warm-up.

My father was a pharmacist, as you know, and his drugstore, while far from prosperous, held up fairly well during the lean years. Even with no doctor near, his fiercely faithful customers brought all prescriptions back to him in Rhame. And, since no one had ever seen a veterinarian, perforce he became the animal expert for a sizeable region. Cattle vaccines were beginning to be used by some ranchers. Plus, odd diseases like sleeping sickness in horses would occasionally bring a rush of customers.

Dad continued to be the source of first aid in the area, splinting and bandaging countless wounds that would have called for stitches anywhere else. He was also the first to be sought for advice. Regularly our wall phone with its hanging receiver would ring in the night.

"These are my symptoms, Hans," would come a plaintive voice. "Am I sick enough that I need to drive to Miles City to the doctor?" Miles City was, of course, 120 miles away.

Anyway, Mother and Dad eked out enough dollars to plan on sending my sister, Adele, and me to Concordia College in Moorhead, Minnesota. Most of Mother's sisters and brothers had gone there and our grandfather had graduated from a sister college. In our staunchly Lutheran family, nothing so heathen as a state college was up for discussion. So, in 1937, Adele was duly driven the 500 miles to far-off Minnesota.

"Things look pretty good this year," farmers had noted in the spring. So crops were planted hopefully, pastures were green, and cattle stopped showing their ribs. Rain fell from the clouds at a normal rate. But clear sailing was too much to expect. Something much more menacing than rain filled the sky that summer. It was grasshoppers.

If you know those insects, you know they are harmless enough. How many times we kids would hold one in our palm and say sternly, "Spit tobacco or I'll kill you," with a mighty feeling of power. We never had to kill one, though. They always brought up a drop of brownish liquid and were allowed to hop away.

This time they were different—much bigger, for one thing. Also, instead of staying on the ground were they belonged, these monsters flew through the atmosphere in vast clouds.

While in high school, I worked in the drugstore after school hours. One warm day in June I remember stepping out to the sidewalk on Main Street.

"What can that be in the sky?" I mused. Folks were doing the same from other stores.

"Looks like a thundercloud, it's so black," I heard from one side.

"Even the air near the ground is full of huge grasshoppers. Awful!" exclaimed another.

"How do we get rid of them? Spray?" someone asked. We all knew *that* was a joke.

For the moment, we could only hope it was a one-time phenomenon. But the next day there came another few million, and the next and the next, all through the summer. Crops were gone, nibbled to the ground. The ravenous hordes even ate prairie grass and chewed the sagebrush. Back slid the region into depression.

Folks at the drugstore soda fountain, always a gathering place, heard little happy talk.

"I never was sorry for those ancient Pharaohs in Egypt before, when God sent them a locust plague," one rancher said mournfully. "Now I know just how they felt."

Our family finances then took another hit. Uncle Nels, who owned the Ford dealership, had taken out a bank loan earlier in the year, confident things were looking up. Dad had no qualms about signing as back-up. Now, with the locust plague, ranchers couldn't pay for those new Ford trucks after all. A good hunk of our college money was needed for the loan. Dad knew he would be repaid, which he was, but that didn't help at the time. Adele had finished only her freshman year.

"Two years apiece is all we can manage," Dad realized, "and even then you girls will have to take all the sideline jobs you can get."

"It's okay for me," Adele maintained cheerfully. "I want to teach elementary school anyway. A two-year degree from a teacher's college will do for that, and I can transfer to one of those next fall. That's all I will need for now."

When my turn came I too headed for Concordia. Luckily the college gave free tuition to valedictorians, which I was. Don't be too impressed, though. There were only fifteen in my class, and few even considered college, so didn't bother to study very hard.

There was no such thing as a government loan in those days. However, the Depression did spawn something called the National Youth Administration. Under that plan students could work for the college itself and apply the meager money they earned toward room and board. My job was in the office of the president of the college, mostly typing and filing (not too efficiently.)

For books and clothes I picked up extra cash by getting the dry cleaning concession for women's dorms, also working in a drug store on Wednesday evenings. Adele, bless her, kept me in spending money by sending $10 a month, though she herself made only $70 a month at her new teaching job.

My first two college years passed in a joyful haze, with summers spent back in the drugstore. Somehow, even another summer of grasshoppers didn't mean total catastrophe. Dad had invested in an ice cream freezer to bump up the fountain business. The idea worked well, and I only occasionally begrudged getting up at 5 a.m. to make the day's supply. It gave me a chance to play with new flavors. Some were successful; some I had to eat myself. I let customers create names—generally, tasty gems such as "jackrabbit tongues" and the like. Other names had to be whispered. Ranchers used earthy language.

I had no way of saving money during those summers. Family members like myself didn't expect to be paid. When my junior year approached, I needed to look for loans. The government was still not into that business, and banks couldn't consider me. I did find a couple of alumni organizations with loan funds. Regretfully, they told me they only accepted boys. Finally a faculty wives' group organized itself to fill that gap and I became more hopeful. Dad came up with a fine idea too.

"I'll tell you what," he proposed. "We have never opened the drugstore on Sunday afternoons, but if you want to do that, and agree to run the place yourself, you can keep all the Sunday fountain proceeds for college."

That sounded great. The drawback was that Sundays were usually pretty slow. I needed to encourage more business, but how? Ranchers' families and cowhands tended to work on Sundays just the same as they did every other day. There had to be an incentive for some of them to come to town.

"My sundaes and sodas are okay," I said to one of the cowboys, "but they aren't enough to make somebody jump into a pickup and drive 15 or 20 miles to town all by themselves. What can I do?"

"You do need a little excitement," he agreed. Then came an inspiration.

"Poker dice!" he declared. "We always shoot dice in the bunkhouse. I'll bring you some."

Next day he was there with five large dice in a sturdy leather shaker about the size of a drinking glass.

"Why don't you shake dice with anybody who wants something from the fountain, free if they win, double if they don't? Odds are you'd come out 50/50 over the length of the summer. I'll bet there would be a lot more business."

"Yes, and when I lose, it will be wholesale, so Dad might pick up some profit out of it too," I added. "Let's go! Want a banana split? I'll roll you double or nothing!"

Fountain business definitely picked up. As the word spread, visiting the Rhame drugstore on Sunday afternoon got to be a regular habit for lots of country folks.

"It's a lot cheaper than the bar, too," ranchers' wives sometimes noted.

"Do I dare tell all my clergy uncles how I am raising college money?" I asked Mother, whose family was loaded with Lutheran ministers. "Will they think it's a sin?"

"They'd be delighted," she insisted. "Gambling may be sinful when it's addictive, but how many people can drink enough malted milks at one time to get hooked? Instead, they would just get sick."

I loved college, all four years of it.

MY WAR WITH THE NORTH ATLANTIC

Do you suppose crossing the North Atlantic aboard a ship carrying 7,000 troops, dodging enemy submarines and braving mid-winter storms, sounds like a fun-filled cruise? Read on and judge for yourself.

During World War II American women were considered too fragile to leave United States soil. Hence, on graduation from college in 1943, with much of the world in conflict, I watched my fellow male students head for military training the minute they left school. Then they spread out to far-off oceans and continents.

"I'd like to go overseas like the guys do," I complained to my roommate. "But if I join the army I can be stationed only in the States."

"Me too," she sighed. "I'm enlisting in the WAVES (the women's navy corps) and they won't even let us sail on a ship."

Not sure what to do, I took a job with General Mills Corporation in Minneapolis. As a food company, it was supposed to be essential to the war effort. The trouble was, my job was to organize advertising campaigns for Wheaties breakfast cereal, which hardly seemed essential to anything except General Mills' profits.

Then one day I saw a tantalizing ad asking if I wanted to be one of a few women who would work for American embassies in North Africa and the eastern Mediterranean. By 1943 those were no longer active war zones. Would I! My response was immediate and, to my surprise, I was accepted. In short order I found myself in Washington, DC ready for six months of training in the State Department.

"Learning how to handle passports and visas is fine," groaned one of the twenty-five women being guided through the intricacies of U.S. Government dealings with foreign countries. "But will we ever learn to code and decode all these intelligence messages?"

"You'd better," responded an instructor. "That will be one of your main jobs." Impressed, back we went to struggle with our cipher machines.

Before long I was informed I had been assigned to the embassy in Cairo, Egypt.

"Sounds wonderful. How am I going to get there?" I wanted to know.

"You, along with those going to other countries, will just have to wait until transport is available," was the response. "We have to depend on the military to go anywhere."

In early February we were told to pack one suitcase for a trip.

"Has anybody heard about what sort of a trip it'll be?" we asked each other.

But in wartime all tongues were silenced. "Loose lips sink ships" was the motto. If anyone had an inkling, she wouldn't have dared mention it.

A few days later, we were put on a train to New York. Next our group was driven to what must have been a pier, though no water was visible. We saw only what seemed to be a massive building, several stories high with few windows, and a series of three or four building-length platforms near the top. On each of these platforms (really decks of a troopship) were hundreds and hundreds of yelling, waving servicemen. I felt like an idiot, one of a group of women wearing high heels and lugging heavy suitcases toward the ramp that would take us on board.

Still, that welcome wasn't so bad. In Washington women had outnumbered men ten to one. Here, on what we learned was the British liner Mauretania, the passenger roll contained 7,000 troops, 150 female Red Cross workers, and 25 State Department personnel. I, for one, didn't mind the change.

"This ship is fast enough to outrun German submarines, so we have no convoy," we were told by fellow passengers once we were on the vessel. "We're supposed to make it to England in less than a week."

England? I thought of the semi-tropical clothes in my suitcase (packed for Egypt, after all) and figured I might have to wear all of them at the same time to stay warm. I was right. Given a small cabin which had once held two, my seven roommates and I shared a bathroom with another eight in the next cabin. This was the height of luxury compared to the enlisted troops, who had to sleep in shifts wherever there was space. Their slumbering bodies filled all available cabins as well as public lounges.

"It will take hours for all 7,000 to be fed," we heard next. "That means only two meals a day."

We weren't allowed to loll around in our cabins, either. Mornings were to be spent in the fresh air. My group was assigned to the top deck, open to cloudy skies and perfectly designed to catch every icy blast of North Atlantic wind.

At first, a brisk circular walk around the deck was possible, even enjoyable. Soon the place got so crowded that the head of the line merged into its rear and the walk became a show shuffle. Sometimes a little open space would appear, and one might try to grab it for some extra mobility. We learned quickly, however, that such space opened up only around generals. It wouldn't do to bump one of those.

Obviously, there was plenty of time for conversation. It was pleasant chatting with guys from a variety of hometowns. Once, four of us attempted to play cards in a sheltered corner. At first we all agreed that it was fun, but before long our fingers were too stiff with cold to hold the cards.

Eventually, hallelujah, the dining hall welcomed us somewhere out of the freezing wind. Our warm respite didn't last long, though, and what was the afternoon's program? Lifeboat drill.

"Good. We won't be stuck on the top deck," one of our group remarked hopefully. "Maybe we'll be sheltered from the wind."

Since, like the other State Department recruits, my only outer wear was a thin raincoat, I was thankful for the added layer of a life jacket, but even that seemed sparse after a few hours.

"Do you realize," asked one sufferer, "where we've been stationed? On a portside deck, facing straight toward the North Pole."

Later we learned our ship had detected the presence of a submarine. The British had sonar before the Germans, hence were warned of danger in time to take appropriate action. We had veered far north, almost to Iceland, to keep out of its path. Instead of being grateful for keeping us safe, if we had known about it, we would likely have complained that the maneuver added a day to our crossing, which meant another 24 hours of Arctic Circle experience, such as toes turning to ice cubes.

Our temperature improved, however, when we were finally allowed back to our cabin. One of my roommates got there first and was jubilant.

"Our bathtub pours out steaming hot seawater," she chortled. "Let's all sit around the edge of the tub and put our feet in. That will thaw us out."

It did a great job.

In the early evening passengers discovered a place to gather even though no public rooms were available: the ship's magnificent staircases.

One experienced Red Cross woman pronounced that it was the best place for group singing she had ever come across. True, we were lopsided with men's voices, but what an echo! Song moved around the ship from one staircase to the next with tremendous enthusiasm. It was a fine way to spend a couple of hours, after which we repaired to our bunks to wait for dawn, when the day's program started over again.

 The only serious problem was the temperature during our daytime hours outside on the decks. We wore pajamas under our clothes and sweaters swathed around our heads.

"Do you think our blood will ever flow normally again?" I asked the shivering body next to me.

"Probably not. I'm just counting the minutes until our hot footbath," was the reply.

One night things looked up. My bunk was a bottom one. In the berth above me was an old State Department hand who had been overseas before. She was fresh from a vacation at her home in Puerto Rico. That night I thought I heard the clink of a bottle. Then came a cautious silence, followed by the unmistakable thump of a cork. Though I didn't detect any glugs, I could picture them vividly. Might it be something like rum or sherry? I wasn't a drinker, but it seemed a great way to warm my chilled innards.

The next day I waited for a chance to find Carmen alone as we tramped the deck.

"Carmen," I said. "I definitely heard bottle sounds coming from your bunk. Cut me in tonight and I won't tell the others."

Carmen agreed readily enough. She confessed she had had an idea what kind of a trip it was going to be. Therefore she had carefully packed several bottles of, yes, rum to make it go more smoothly. I think she really had been wanting to share.

"You know, there's no way to keep this a secret in our tiny cabin," she sighed.

I had a brilliant thought. Why not pass the rum around at that most crucial time of day—the blood-congealed moment when we came in from the frigid blasts and shared our tub of foaming hot water?

That did it. I can't say the rum improved the weather, but it made a huge difference in our attitude toward it. Somehow the voyage was transformed from an ordeal into a reasonably pleasant experience. We could now look forward to a glorious moment of warmth, inside and out, at the end of our frozen days.

When we finally got to the camp in England where we were to wait for the next part of our journey, we were sometimes asked by soldiers how our trip across the Atlantic had been. Any one of us would readily answer, "It was great!"

WAR GAMES ON THE MEDITERRANEAN

Now comes the second half of my World War II cruise. This time we Department of State seafarers found ourselves plying the waves escorted by a convoy of the British Navy. Watching enemy aircraft overhead and trying to keep steady when our ship's depth charges exploded was part of shipboard life. On the plus side were the sunny weather and deep blue of the Mediterranean. A minus was the challenge to our wits and strength by the Brits. Which won? Again, you be the judge.

Between the two voyages was a ten-day sojourn in England.

"Where can we be docking?" we passengers asked each other as the Mauretania pulled up to a pier that February evening.

None of us could see any signs at all. The answer was that, fearful of enemy spies, no street markers, road signs or any other indication of location throughout the country could be discerned. England, in early 1944, had become an immense staging area for the Allied invasion of Europe, which took place the following June. Meanwhile, the air war continued, with its deadly daily toll of bombings and crashes on both sides of the channel.

"Somebody says this is Liverpool," came a whispered report, but we didn't have a chance to explore. Instead we were whisked off into the night by train. Six of us crowded into a compartment.

"We women are being sent to a U.S. Army camp to wait for passage the rest of the way to the Middle East," a passenger confided somewhat smugly. "One of the officers told me."

"Maybe there will be heat in the barracks," another commented wistfully as we pulled our thin coats around us on the chilly train. Obviously, power was being saved to fight the war.

An hour or so later, a short truck ride brought us to our appointed goal. It turned out to be a "Replacement Depot" camp providing temporary housing for "floaters" who hadn't yet been assigned to a specific unit. I guess those troops weren't expected to stay long. The blackout-curtained room to which the twenty-five of us were shown certainly made no attempt to be cozy. Its only furniture was a series of three-tiered metal bunks. A bathroom boasted a couple of showers and a few sinks, but no hint of warmth in either air or water. After we freshened up as best we could, a soldier led to through the darkness to a dining room.

What a contrast! Lights were bright, warmth was heavenly. The supreme spirit-lifter was a large and enthusiastic army orchestra rendering lively swing tunes, straight from the airways of home. I'll never forget the number the band was playing as the door opened and the music enveloped us: U.S. band leader Johnny Long's arrangement of "Shanty Town." If you weren't around in the early 1940's you may not have heard it, but this rendition was the very latest thing. It was as unexpected as a reception by General Eisenhower himself—and much more welcome.

Gloom was gone and chills forgotten for our ten days at that army camp. Every meal was shared with soldiers, to rhythms that made blood flow and feet tap. Tunes by Glenn Miller, Benny Goodman and other rousing orchestras could be heard via loudspeakers all over the area. What a great way to boost morale during the months of waiting before the invasion.

Then we were back to the docks of Liverpool and another ship, a real switch from the first. Again it was a former British passenger liner, but much smaller and with fewer troops. This time the troops were British, both men and women. Six of us were assigned to a cabin far larger than our former one. Also, wondrously, the luxurious lounges were available to passengers.

Once at sea, we could discern some of the other ships in our convoy.

"Is that an aircraft carrier?" I asked, and made out a small one, along with freighters and destroyers. The ships kept changing positions, so we couldn't get used to having the same neighbor for long.

"The decks are really roomy," was the relieved comment of the first of our group. "Now we can get decent exercise." Also, after turning out of the Atlantic and into the Mediterranean, the air seemed positively balmy.

"This is a cruise we are really going to enjoy," was the common belief.

What we didn't expect was the British penchant for playing games. Also, some authority had determined that passengers should be kept busy every waking second. Calisthenics and lifeboat drills were no problem, but who would have expected to be the American team in all sort of nutty games?

"Have you heard what we are doing this morning?" A roommate asked on our second day. "They're having a quiz show, and we Americans are expected to make up some of the competing teams."

We worked our way to a large auditorium below decks.

"This may not turn out to be fun," sighed one of our number.

How right she was! Our American contingent was in wildly over our heads. Questions had been sent in from all over the ship, and showed in a hurry how different English education was from ours.

I well remember my first question: "Who was the first man to climb the Matterhorn?"

I thought I was pretty good even to have heard of the Matterhorn itself. That was no help as my ignominious "I don't know" was broadcast to the entire ship. Of course the climber turned out to be an Englishman, Sir Wallace Wimpole by name, but now that I know the answer, no one has ever asked me.

The other contestants fared little better.

"We should have been asked to submit questions too," we groused, back in our cabins. "How about if we asked 'What is the capital of Nevada?' Let's see how the Brits would handle that one."

Oh well, being superior to Americans may have made the troops feel better. So we did our part, meekly going to the slaughter every morning at quiz hour and not doing much better with the games that followed.

Every afternoon brought an athletic event. At each of those our opponents, British military females, easily proved their superior conditioning. At tug-of-war, for instance, all 25 of us were at one end of an enormous rope extending much of the length of one deck. We clung mightily, but were pulled over the line in such a rush we almost went overboard. Ball games, versions of soccer (whoever heard of soccer in North Dakota?) were worse.

"I don't think there are many more games they can dream up," one optimist opined. Just when we figured there were no more ways to be humbled, though, new ones appeared. Who would have expected to need to shine at throwing darts? Still, we decided our role was to be game for every challenge, however abject the humiliation. Soon the troops loudly cheered our briefest moments of success.

Intense fighting was raging on the Italian peninsula while Allied bombers and fighters struggled to bomb and strafe Nazi Europe from bases there. On the Mediterranean, however, there was not much warlike activity. Though an occasional Italian plane appeared overhead, apparently their pilots decided the menace of our convoy aircraft carrier wasn't worth taking a risk on, so no bombs dropped on any of our vessels.

Some years later I met a Navy guy who had been on a destroyer in an American convoy on that route in the same month. His convoy had lost two ships.

Another hazard was when our own ship would expel an anti-submarine depth charge with an explosion that shook the walls around us. One night I was tossed out of my upper bunk by a particularly close explosion, which also broke most of the ship's mirrors. Strangely enough, no one on board seemed to take any of this at all seriously. The eternal optimism of youth, I guess.

The day came when we reached Port Said, Egypt. There, amid friendly waves and cheerful goodbyes from our fellow passengers, who were going through the Suez Canal and on to the Far East, we Americans disembarked.

All in all, it was an extraordinary journey from New York to Egypt in the midst of the carnage of the worst of wars.

MY FAVORITE HOLIDAY

For some, Christmas or Thanksgiving is the holiday to savor. For me, it's the Fourth of July. My special Fourth came in 1944, two days after I turned twenty-two.

It was less than a month after the American and British invasion of Europe on the Normandy beaches. After some rough going, our troops were at last out of the surf and progressing into France. Allied countries finally dared to feel some optimism after years of uncertainty.

I was in Cairo. It had once been customary for the embassy there to have an Independence Day party for all Americans in the area.

"This seems an excellent year to revive the idea," the ambassador had announced. "There may not be many American civilians around, but there are plenty of troops."

True. An enormous U.S. Air Force base was at the edge of the city, plus a sizeable army enclave and hospital. In addition, large numbers of men were always there on leave from the difficult grind of fighting in Italy.

Our embassy itself was small, a three-story villa in a section of Cairo known as Garden City, a few blocks from the Nile River.

"Fortunately, we have this large garden," we staffers agreed. "And in Egypt we never have to worry about rain."

That was true too. In some years, one could take an afternoon nap and sleep through the entire rainy season. Moisture to support the country came entirely by way of the Nile River.

Indeed, the garden did look lovely in the twilight, with strings of lights and tables of food and drink. Handsome Egyptian waiters wore floor-length white garments accented by wide red sashes. Note that I say "twilight." No daytime affair would have been possible under the scorching desert sun of July.

The embassy staff was small too: eight men and five women. We were to function as greeters and hosts for however many guests might appear.

"I think I've already welcomed a couple hundred at the gate," I murmured to my replacement at that station. Still, the garden wasn't overcrowded. There was a holiday atmosphere as we Americans, all of us far from home, took pleasure in each other's company.

One man, Arnold Stebinger (called "Steb," he told me) caught my attention more than any of the others. He was somewhat unusual in that he was wearing civilian clothes. I learned that he was working for Mobil Oil Company, which supplied the fuel for both air force and army bases. A foot badly mangled in a childhood accident had kept him from acceptance into any of the military services.

"Sorry, I'm not allowed to linger with any one guest," I said regretfully after we had chatted a few minutes. I couldn't accept his invitation to go out after the party either, because I already had a date with the correspondent for Columbia Broadcasting. American women were scarce in Cairo so we rarely had a free evening. Not that you would hear me complain.

Never one to waste time, Steb phoned the next day.

"How about joining me and a group of friends for a moonlight picnic beyond the pyramids?"

It was lovely. The following day the phone rang again.

"Interested in going with me to a sailboat party on the Nile?" Clearly he knew how to entertain a girl. Could I resist?

The attraction was mutual. At Thanksgiving we were engaged.

"It's too bad we can't meet each other's families," we agreed. "But how can we know when the war will be over?"

In fact, we had no idea when, if ever, we would be able to get off the continent of Africa. So, the following year, we were married in the Anglican Cathedral in Cairo. In lieu of my father, the ambassador gave me away.

Looking back after 58 years together, that Fourth of July was indeed an auspicious point in time.

Now move to 1980 A.D., thirty-five years after the event. Steb and I were spending a weekend in Charleston, South Carolina, USA, with two other couples. By that time he had retired from Mobil and was teaching in the Masters in International Business program at the University of South Carolina. The other two men were faculty members also.

Over cocktails one evening, we three couples, all long married, got to talking about where each of us had met the other. Steb and I were used to having the most exotic example, so when it came to our turn, we duly recalled that evening at the embassy garden in Cairo.

This time, one of the other men spoke up.

"I'll be darned," he said, thinking back. "*I* was at that party."

He had been in the crew of an air transport plane flying across northern Africa to Cairo's air base. They had arrived in Egypt that afternoon.

Someone had said, "There's a party at the embassy tonight. Want to go?"

"Why not?" he responded, whereupon they located a car and driver. Eventually they found Garden City, where Americans were gathered.

"It was a beautiful evening," he remembered. "Great food, great drinks. Just not enough girls."

THE PRESIDENT AND I

They say lying never pays. Maybe it shouldn't, or maybe the fib I told wasn't as black as some. Anyway, it led me to a brief involvement with the President and the Secretary of State of the United States, plus two kings and an emperor. Not bad for one exaggeration about a class I had taken in high school.

Rhame High School, as you may remember, had only some fifty students. Few of them expected to go to college, so the School Board tried to provide some vocational training. Thus, during one of my years there, a teacher arrived to instruct us in shorthand and typing.

Typing was no problem, but it quickly became clear the teacher was a complete novice at shorthand. She didn't learn fast either. For the entire semester, teacher and students together puzzled our way through the Gregg Shorthand text.

"This is like learning cuneiform," a fellow student muttered. "I can memorize the strokes pretty well. Stringing a bunch of them together, though, is hopeless."

Another agreed. " But when I try to read back what I've written, all those squiggles are, well, just squiggles."

When I applied for a job with the American Embassy in Cairo, one of the questions had been whether I could take shorthand. Hoping the little I had learned would come back to me when I needed it, I bravely answered yes.

It wasn't a problem for a long time. None of the Foreign Service officers was given to dictating. They preferred careful drafts in longhand of their intelligence reports to State Department headquarters in Washington. Foreign Service *officers,* incidentally, could be only men in those days; women had to be Foreign Service *clerks.*

Sometimes I was asked to substitute for the ambassador's secretary, who had an occasional alcohol problem. The ambassador did, in fact, dictate. He spoke very, very slowly, however. I could jot down his actual words with time to spare.

Then came a fateful Sunday when it was my turn to be on duty. Our normal embassy work schedule was eight hours a day, six days a week, plus every third Sunday. On that day one officer and one clerk had extra duty. Activity was light on Sunday usually. My job was mostly to decipher messages coming in over the code machines.

That Sunday morning one message I decoded took my breath away.

I raced to tell the day's officer.

"Get this!" I yelled. "It says President Roosevelt is coming here. What's more, he arrives a week from today!"

We re-read the cable together. This was shortly after World War II had finally ended, and It announced that President Franklin D. Roosevelt, then meeting with Winston Churchill of England and Josef Stalin of Russia at Yalta, would be coming to Egypt. Would we please arrange for meetings between him and three heads of state: King Farouk of Egypt, King Ibn Saud of Saudi Arabia, and Emperor Haile Selassie of Ethiopia.

We phoned the ambassador to come immediately. The three of us went into high gear. Because of the danger of assassination, all activity had to be kept strictly secret. That meant we had to attend to every detail ourselves.

"You two contact the embassies in Saudi Arabia and Ethiopia," the ambassador decided. "I'll get hold of the generals of the American Army in North Africa and the American Air Force. A huge collection of dignitaries and their staffs will soon be descending on us here in Egypt. The armed services are the only ones who can handle security and transportation both."

By Monday morning the ambassador's office had become command headquarters. One of my tasks was to code and decode cables and telegrams, which flew fast and thick. My main function, however, was to keep minutes of the almost constant meetings at which the group (plus a Navy Commander who was President Roosevelt's aide-de-camp) decided how to handle events.

"The President himself is to remain on the Navy destroyer which will bring him from Yalta," we were informed by Roosevelt's aide. "His ship will proceed through the Suez Canal to the Bitter Lakes, which lie between the Canal and the Red Sea. There he will receive his guests."

The group had to decide in which order these state visits would occur, plus how to transport and house the participants. They even had to determine which state gifts the President should give. If you want to know what these gifts were, it was an airplane apiece for King Ibn Saud and King Farouk and a jeep for Emperor Haile Selassie. I heard afterward that the latter was miffed over his inferior present.

Unfortunately, the moment arrived when one of the Generals decided to dictate a letter. Then came the inevitable words.

"Miss Ahlness, will you read it back, please?"

The room was silent as the moment of truth came for my Rhame High School shorthand. I drew a long breath and looked at what I had scrawled.

Somehow I must have stumbled through my squiggles, though my memory is mercifully dim. At least, by that time, I had had practice translating my cuneiform into secret code for telegrams. The difference was that with those earlier messages I never had an audience.

The week went by in a daze. We weren't even unduly bothered when the Secretary of State and his entourage blew in with only a couple of hours' notice.

"Thank goodness the secret is finally out," a harassed Cecil Lyon and I agreed. "Now the rest of the embassy staff can stay here with us until after midnight. There's bound to be a mountain of new stuff for us to do with this second crowd."

Fascinating details came from the President's ship. Ibn Saud's visit, especially, was like a page out of *The Arabian Nights*. He came on an American destroyer from Saudi Arabia. Never having been on such a trip before, he and his party refused to sleep in the cabins fixed for them or eat the food prepared on the ship. The poor crew was at wit's end, for the good king and his retinue pitched their tents on the forecastle, slaughtered their sheep on the poop deck and brewed their coffee in the ammunition shafts. Besides the regular run of bodyguards, political advisors, interpreters, etc., the king brought with him his royal fortune teller and astrologer, ceremonial coffee servers and countless other functionaries including eight miscellaneous slaves and scullions. Their robes and headdresses were wonders to behold. More gold was draped over the clothes of the bodyguard than I ever expect to encounter again.

The Emperor of Ethiopia came up on a U.S. Air Force plane, so there wasn't room for such a host of attendants in his case. He did very well for himself, though, and brought as many as could get crammed on board. His prestige demanded large following on any trip.

I was given numerous pictures of the week's proceedings in the Bitter Lakes, which is how I know about the trappings. When I showed them to Rifai, our cook, he was overwhelmed. For hours he went around muttering *"Yah Salaam"*, which means *"Praise be to Allah"*.

When it was all over, I got a Citation from the Secretary of State's office thanking me for my contribution.

Wouldn't the Rhame High School shorthand teacher have been amazed?

LIFE IN EGYPT, DOGGONE IT

Have you ever lived with a psychotic dog? Steb and I did.

It was 1946. We were renting a furnished apartment in Cairo, Egypt, where Steb continued to work for Mobil after the war. One day we were offered the use of a lovely house in a suburb for several months.

"How can we turn it down?" I exulted.

"Don't forget," cautioned Steb. "The offer includes taking care of Shandy."

Sandy, an Airedale dog, was not unknown to us. We had been at her owners' house for dinner one time when conversation was interrupted by loud noises. Clearly they were dog noises, but not the usual ones. It was more a combination of joyful yips, loud slurps and, possibly, hiccups.

"Don't let it bother you," soothed our hostess. "That's just Shandy having imaginary puppies behind the couch."

Once moved in, we learned about another of Shandy's offbeat ideas— that she could catch a crow. An attractive garden extended from the back of the house. It consisted of a lawn, flower beds, and trees, surrounded by a high wall. Because Shandy needed to be kept from roaming, her owner had rigged a long wire between two opposite sides of the wall. Her collar could be connected to the wire, giving her considerable running space.

The trouble was, one of the neighborhood crows figured out a way to tease her. It would swoop down over her head, then fly just ahead of her nose while she chased frenziedly behind, stopped only by a crash into the wall at the end. As soon as she staggered to her feet, the crow would fly back the other direction, Shandy tearing after, until the inevitable collision on the other side. Did the crow ever tire of teasing?

No. And did Shandy ever realize she would never catch up? No. Anyway, they both got exercise, and Shandy was never bothered by her crashes.

"If only I could solve the problem of dogs and birds on watering days," I moaned to a neighbor, who also had a dog. "Have you found any solution?" But nobody had.

Watering days should really have been called "flooding days." Being Egypt, there was never any rain. Once a week we suburbanites had our gardens flooded by means of a tank truck and large hose. It was water from the Nile River. That liquid was so filthy the vegetables had to be sectioned off and watered from our purified household supply. The rest of the garden became a sheet of very muddy water for much of a day.

There was no way to keep hysterical Shandy indoors. I gave up and let her roll in it, which she did, happily, for hours on end. Naturally, she ended up with enough mud on her fur to require multiple baths.

"I wonder what the owners thought of watering day when they decorated all the rooms in white," I groused, dragging her through the house to the bathtub at the end of her orgy.

That wasn't the only problem. Right on schedule, her friend the crow arrived and entered into the sport. Alternately dipping for a bath and shaking its feathers overhead, muddy drops would always land on porch furniture. Watering the garden, then dealing with the aftermath, was a two-day affair.

An Airedale is a large dog and needs lots of exercise. One day I came up with a plan to take Shandy for a run while I rode my bike. But this wasn't as straightforward as one might think.

The Nile River produces a narrow green strip of fertile land on either side of its banks. The rest of the country of Egypt is desert. In our area, all the grassy land on one side of the river was covered by our suburb. In laying out the street plan, no provision had been made for sidewalks or walking paths. Trucks, cars, bicycles, donkey carts and pedestrians all went down the middle of the streets. In addition, this being shortly after World War II, a New Zealand Army camp lay in the desert at one end of town. Its vehicles plowed through the roads with the rest of the traffic, but twice as fast.

"Obviously, this is no place to walk a dog," I thought.

Our house, helpfully, was near the desert, so Shandy, the bike and I could work our way out there for our excursions. The desert surface was not soft and sandy, but was covered by a surprisingly firm crust, so I had a good ride. Shandy absolutely loved it, racing over the sand in glorious freedom.

What I had not foreseen was that Shandy would come into heat.

One inevitable morning, our little caravan was suddenly popular with the wild desert dogs living in the area. First a couple of them came sniffing around Shandy, then others arrived from all directions. These canines (called "pye" dogs) have lived in the desert for centuries, maybe even millennia. Muslims generally dislike dogs, and rarely have them for pets. Yet pye dogs play a useful role as scavengers and aren't hunted. Though wild and scruffy, they are not dangerous. I had never been concerned about them on our outings.

This time was different. Shandy didn't mind the attention. I knew, however, how unpopular I would be with our landlords if their precious pet should become pregnant by a pye dog. I grabbed the leash I had used to get Shandy through the earlier traffic.

"Come on, Shandy," I pleaded. Fastening her to my handlebars, I headed for town as fast as I could, pye dogs in our wake.

Shandy had other ideas. With a sudden jerk, she managed to pull her head out of her collar and joined the dogs of the desert. Leaving my bike, I chased after on foot calling frantically for her to come back. She seemed to get the idea, and actually stopped not far away from me, whereupon she was promptly surrounded by the rest of the animals. Not wanting to give them a chance to start anything, I threw stones to break up their gathering until they were on the move again. This procedure went on for what seemed hours. Shandy and company ran away while I tore after them. Then I pelted them with rocks when they stood still, all the while pleading with Shandy to come back to me.

Incredibly, she finally did.

"From now on, you're going to have to settle for the exercise you get with the crow," I told her sternly. As for me, I had had enough aerobics to last for weeks.

Leave it to Shandy to add drama to our final days in the house. The months had passed, during which we got used to her occasional sessions of producing non-existent pups. Finally Steb and I were to move back into the city. With us would go our furniture ordered from the States, which had been stored in the basement of the rented house.

It was then November and, like a good corporate wife, I was to have some of the other Americans in Cairo to the house for Thanksgiving dinner. As a fairly new bride, I had no idea how to cook any of it myself. We had a cook, however, a tall Sudanese man named Achmed. Several menacing scars embellished each of his cheeks to show his tribal affiliation. His family had been left behind in the Sudan, where he faithfully sent most of his salary.

A good cook, and by this time a good friend, he was even pals with Shandy, Muslim or not.

"She seems to be acting strangely," he told me one morning. "I wonder if she might actually be expecting puppies."

Horrors! How could it have happened? Had someone left the garden gate open? Hurriedly, I called the vet to come and look at her.

We were to be eleven for Thanksgiving dinner. Since Egyptian turkeys tend to be scrawny, Achmed and I ordered two of the largest we could find. They arrived, headless and plucked, a couple of days in advance. Then Achmed dashed from the kitchen.

"The refrigerator stopped running," he gasped. "What shall we do?"

We hauled out all the small picnic iceboxes available, filled them with ice and strewed them over the kitchen and hall. We could only hope these would keep the turkeys and other ingredients fresh until the kerosene refrigerator was fixed. Then I started phoning everyone I knew to see if I could find someone to repair that ailing appliance.

Next, the gardener came racing upstairs to say the hot water pipe had burst in the basement. That was where our furniture was stored, awaiting a crating crew that was supposed to come that very day and haul it away. By the time the three of us got the water turned off (but the mess not cleaned up) a small horde of men had duly arrived.

This furniture crew was energetic enough, but couldn't work in the now-muddy basement. They proceeded to tramp around the house tracking dirt and muck. Eventually I organized an assembly line so they could get the furniture out with as little mud distribution as possible, and do the crating in the yard.

Amidst all of this, Steb unfortunately had a bad cold, and was feeling rotten.

"You have simply got to stay home in bed," I had persuaded him that morning. He must have felt really terrible, because he agreed. In the afternoon I was getting worried about him and called the local doctor. That worthy announced Steb had bronchitis and started him on sulfa (this was before antibiotics) and large quantities of cough medicine.

While ice melted over the kitchen floor, I spent most of the Wednesday morning before Thanksgiving rushing around town trying to find someone who could repair the refrigerator. Achmed predicted that he would have to have one of the turkeys cooked in someone else's kitchen. With ours so cluttered, he couldn't get enough helpers into it to do all the preparation.

"Hooray, I found someone to look at the refrigerator," I exclaimed finally, bringing into the kitchen a man I had managed to hire. But he didn't stay long. He said he needed new parts and would have to take a train to Cairo to buy them.

Steb, during all this, was upstairs in bed gulping sulfa and feeling steadily worse. He gasped and wheezed and was having an awful time breathing. I was positive he had pneumonia. I couldn't take his temperature, though. The thermometer was packed with our other belongings, now hauled away in their new crates. The doctor seemed to have disappeared off the face of the earth. Shandy didn't help either, loping around looking woebegone. She also insisted on remaining underfoot wherever I might be.

There was no direction things could go except up, which, happily, they began to do.

The doctor reappeared and came to the house after dinner that evening. This time he looked at Steb and said, "This is an asthma attack, not bronchitis after all."

He thereupon administered a shot of adrenaline, which cleared up Steb's breathing in fifteen minutes and left him with nothing worse than a few coughs and sniffles.

Thanksgiving morning, the repairman brought new insides for the refrigerator, which promptly started making ice again, while a second man appeared with a new pipe to fit the hot water system in the basement.

Meantime, Achmed decided he wouldn't need extra help after all. By the time our guests arrived for Thanksgiving dinner at one p.m., the place looked as though things had been running smoothly forever.

Dinner was super, Steb breathed nicely, and I could actually enjoy the party. Then, to add one last drop to our overflowing cup, the vet came Friday morning.

Shandy is definitely not pregnant," he proclaimed. "She has nothing troubling her but worms. I can treat those easily."

This story has a postscript, though. Guess what turned out to be the cause of Steb's asthma? Dog hair.

INTO BEIRUT

If you want a break from your routine, try moving to a country which uses two languages, neither of which you speak. Add narrow mountain roads where drivers pass only on curves, and a food market where you have to bargain for every string bean. Now you know how dazed I felt in Beirut, Lebanon. Getting used to it was an adventure.

Steb and I were the envy of everyone we knew in the Middle East when we were stationed there in 1947. World War II's horrors had barely touched its shores, so Beirut immediately resumed its pre-war role as a sophisticated international center. Casinos opened, some in gorgeous seaside locations. Others were on stunning mountain tops. Rich Arabs from the Persian Gulf mingled at night clubs with Lebanese women in the latest Paris fashions. All of us were entertained by cabaret performers hailing straight from Europe.

"Whatever happened to those Arab meals I've read about in books?" I asked after our first month. "You know, the kind with a whole roasted lamb in the middle of the table, where you are offered the eye of a sheep as the greatest delicacy."

Instead there were "intimate" Lebanese dinners for twenty people, where we were served eight or nine courses of French cuisine.

During wartime, every woman in my world had worn knee-length dresses, presumably to save cloth for military uniforms. At a moment in late 1947, however, a couturier in France named Christian Dior brought out what he called the "new look." Dress lengths instantly dropped to the instep. It wasn't a month later that Steb and I went to a dinner party where every single Lebanese woman was decked to the anklebone. They wore outfits with feathers, sloping shoulders—the Dior works. We dowdy Americans and British cowered above our still-bare knees and calves.

The women in country villages were nowhere near as chic. They wore the same shapeless full-length garments as in centuries before. No veils though. I had seen no women in Egypt wearing them, and the same was true for Lebanon and Syria. Nothing at all on the female head was the norm for most of the Middle East in the 1940's.

"Let's explore the mountains," Steb had proposed soon after we arrived there.

So we did, in spite of the absence of maps and the unsettling width of most roads. Those were never much wider than our car itself. Steb relished the challenge. Personally, I would have enjoyed the views more if my eyes hadn't been closed in terror much of the time. Originally goat tracks, then donkey paths, roads routinely had on one side sheer drops of hundreds of feet. Turning the car around couldn't even be contemplated except in a village, and then it was questionable.

"The road has disappeared," I pointed out in one village when our route seemed to stop altogether.

"No, look," he answered. "They've just put steps into it."

Luckily, the steps were wide ones, which Steb calmly drove down until he reached the road going out the other side of the hamlet.

Villagers were invariably friendly and hospitable. We could have had a meal with them at any time. They would often delightedly show us ruins, too, of what might have been anything from Roman to Byzantine to Turkish structures, for all we (or they) knew.

Inevitably, the day came when we had a flat tire from something we picked up near a group of houses. Steb hauled the jack out of the trunk and shoved it under the axle.

What a sensation as he pumped the wheel off the ground! Every man in the community stood around, marveling at his strength as he lifted the car all by himself.

In the meantime, I chatted with local women and was shown the pride of the village—a treadle Singer sewing machine. When they demonstrated how their marvel worked, I exclaimed dutifully. I was careful not to mention the electric table model I had at home.

Then back to the car where Steb was modestly accepting praise for his unusual powers. Not only did he raise the car, but took a tire off and put the whole thing together again. We left amid echoes of mutual admiration.

Indeed, daily lessons in Arabic and French were beginning to pay off.

THE MOST FASCINATING PLACE IMAGINABLE

For a history buff, it was hard to beat Beirut as the world's top choice for a spot to live. It has a heavenly location at the end of the blue Mediterranean. Directly behind tower 10,000-foot mountains, their slopes once covered by the fabled cedars of Lebanon whose wood framed Solomon's temple. For added magic, it lies beside St. George's Bay. There St. George supposedly killed the dragon, making the sea safe for swimmers ever after.

Steb and I moved to Beirut shortly after World War II. Lebanon had been an independent country for only a couple of years but had not forgotten its days as mighty Phoenicia. Back then its seafarers were the foremost explorers of the ancient world and its people used mankind's first alphabet.

"You can't imagine what I've found!" I told Steb after my first expedition out of town. "Beside a pass near the Dog River there's a cliff face with inscriptions carved into it. Guess who left the first one?"

Barely waiting for his "I've no idea," I burbled on. "Our old pal from Egypt, Ramses II!"

Indeed, Ramses II, a pharaoh who lived about 1250 B.C. had been a ubiquitous figure. He built many beautiful temples, as well as statues of himself, all over Egypt. Even when he hadn't, he scratched out the name of the actual builder (on the Sphinx, for instance) and replaced it with his own.

"He says (in hieroglyphics) that he fought against the Hittites farther up the coast," I reported from my guidebook. "Naturally he declared it a great victory. The carving of an enormous pile of left hands shows how many men his army slaughtered."

Next to lead an army over the pass and leave a message about it was an Assyrian, Tiglath-Pileser by name, who duly recorded his exploits (in cuneiform) around 800 B.C.

"After that came a carving by Nebuchadnezzar himself!" I said excitedly. "It's as if he walked right out of my long-ago Sunday School lessons!"

Close by were the records (in Greek) of a couple of Greek battalions, which would have been still before the Christian era. After that, Romans turned up (using Latin). Then a number of centuries passed. No crusaders used the cliff for self-promotion, but Turks did a little later, leaving several messages (in Turkish and Arabic) over some hundreds of years. They even built a bridge nearby which is still standing. The last, in historic sequence, was inscribed by an Australian regiment (in English at last!) It tells of passing that way in the fight against the Ottoman Empire in World War I. Surely this is the most amazing first-hand record in history, stretching over more than thirty centuries.

Those inscriptions were just the beginning of an exploration of the country's antiquities. Lebanese mountains shielded remains of buildings from every era.

Steb's favorite was the site of a temple to Adonis and Astarte, ancient gods of fertility. The reason he liked it was the location. High on a mountain was a grotto, reached on foot after the hair-raising road dwindled to a complete end. Though dry in fall and winter, water gushed from the grotto in spring when snow melted on the peaks. In steamy July, when we visited, it tumbled down the mountainside to form an inviting pool.

"Eeee!" I screeched on my first contact, having made the large mistake of jumping right in. I got out fast.

"Does anyone have a thermometer in his pack?" Somebody did; it was 46 degrees. So much for swimming.

Steb read from the guidebook that a large temple had been built there with granite pillars brought from a quarry 700 miles down the Nile in Egypt.

"How in the world did they haul them to this remote spot?" he wondered.

"It's astonishing what the search for fertility will produce," mused another of our party. Scattered building stones still covered a wide area.

"What can these be?" questioned one of the women, indicating bits of cloth tied to branches of trees and bushes.

"Things haven't changed," commented a more knowledgeable picnicker. "Infertile twentieth century women are still making their entreaties to the gods."

Romans were tireless builders, and left at Baalbeck (in the valley between mountains of Lebanon and Syria) some famous temples to which I, in my "company wife" role, took innumerable visitors. My supreme compliment came the day Arab guides there simply didn't bother attempting to escort my party. Instead, they smilingly ushered us into the temple precincts, acknowledging that I had been there almost as often as they had.

The best of the Roman remains, to my mind, was a whole city, built in what now seems the craziest place imaginable—a dreary desert valley halfway between Damascus and Baghdad. To get there a group of us chartered a plane, landed on the closest semi-flat ground we could find, and taxied a mile or more to the city.

"In its time, this was the edge of empire," one of our travelers told us. "Queen Zenobia was its ruler. Romans were the overlords."

"I'm not sure who it was built to impress, but this is 2000 years later and it sure impresses *me*", commented another. The ruins stretched for more than a mile.

The old marketplace, forum, senate, pink marble amphitheatre and principal temple still stood. Beyond them the layout of streets was clear because they were lined on both sides with graceful stone columns, stretching across the plain. Littering the ground were beautifully carved pieces of cornice and frieze. We walked through a dense field of delicate sculptures and occasional toga-clad busts of eminent citizens, now headless.

Much as I would have loved to take home one of the carved pieces of stone, it seemed more fitting to leave them there in silent witness to the splendor of an antique city.

The Trans-Arabian Pipeline, a huge engineering project to bring oil from the Persian Gulf fields to the Mediterranean, was built during our years there. The project director and his wife were neighbors of ours, so we and the Chandlers went on an excursion one Sunday to check its progress.

"The minute we got out of desert country and into Lebanon we started uncovering antiquities," Bill told us. "Work on the pipeline has been interrupted constantly while Lebanese archeologists decide whether to move them to a museum, and even more of them were unearthed as we neared the Phoenician port of Sidon."

"Right over there," he pointed, "we uncovered the entire mosaic floor of a spacious Byzantine church. Work had to be halted completely so the floor could be transferred piece by piece to the National Museum in Beirut. And then, only a few feet below that floor there was another one!"

The church had rested on a lovely slope in the foothills of the mountains. It's no wonder the spot had been picked twice for a major building.

"One archeologist said that ten feet of dirt could account for a time span of many centuries," Bill told us. "Our head office in the States is in constant agonies over what might appear next. I'll admit I never expected to work on a project where ancient stones are more of a challenge than the engineering."

Crusaders had come in their zeal to retake the Holy Land, and their castles lasted much longer than their fighters did. Perched on spectacular crags, some of them were still keeping guard over a river far below, or a lonely mountain pass.

An expedition to one of them brought us to an enormous walled castle still almost intact. It was so big that a village had grown up in one of its courtyards. Graceful stone chapels and arches looked as if they had been constructed only recently. Even the moat and the innermost keep were little changed from the time of those fervent religious wars.

"Present-day village children must really enjoy the winding stairways and hidden rooms within the walls," one of our explorers commented. "Wouldn't you have loved those arrow slots to peek out on the way to crenellated turrets when you were a kid?"

Another said he had heard that there were still blue-eyed children living in the area. I guess there are lots of ways to make history.

HOW TO BECOME AN EXPERT ON LABOR PAINS

New babies are wonderful. Their births are rightly celebrated by grandparents, aunts and uncles, friends and neighbors. Parents know, however, that before babies there come something called labor pains. As a producer of babies in three different cultures, I consider myself something of an authority.

First there was our son Jimmy, born in Beirut, Lebanon in 1949. Amazingly, the pains started the morning of the very day he was due. By afternoon Steb and I headed for the hospital. An American doctor was head of obstetrics there and I had been seeing him throughout the pregnancy. However, he had gone to Aleppo, Syria, that day. A Lebanese doctor met us and led us to a hospital room.

In the corridor, a small cluster of people was sitting outside the doors of most rooms.

"How can they be so unperturbed with all that yelling and screaming coming from inside the rooms?" we asked each other nervously. The doctor was calm and showed us to a pleasant chamber. He said he would be back to check on me as soon as it was necessary.

Hours passed, with pains increasing in severity. We managed all right, with Steb vigorously flapping a hand-held fan to cool me off as each pain hit.

Eventually, close to midnight, I told Steb I thought something drastic was about to happen. He rushed out and brought the doctor, who appeared quite annoyed with me.

"Why did you wait so long to let me know about this?" he asked.

"We thought you were going to come and check," I answered.

"But you didn't scream, or even yell," he responded. "Naturally we thought your pains had stopped and you were sleeping."

So much for Lebanese rules. I did redeem myself, however, by having a boy, much superior to a girl, apparently. Steb was inundated with praises. The card on one of our many baskets of flowers summed it up: "Congratulations on your *son*," it read, "and your elevation in the sight of the people."

Our next child, Anne, was born courtesy of England's National Health Service. The place was the grandly-named "Elizabeth Garrett Anderson Maternity Hospital" in London. Though the birth facilities were carefully egalitarian, it was possible to get a private room by paying a little extra.

We opted for that and were shown to the top floor, where I arrived with an armload of paperback thrillers. Knowing the hours of waiting in store, I was primed with exciting page-turners. The idea was, as much as possible, to keep the mind off labor pains. They also worked as a way to pass the time in the early and middle stages, which actually used up most of the hours.

Steb was summarily told to leave.

"It seems husbands aren't welcome," he said plaintively. "Who is going to be on hand to flap a fan?"

I got settled with one of my books, but a nurse came in and changed my plans.

"All delivery rooms are on the floor below," she announced. "They are reached by elevator. We don't want to take any chances on elevator service, so you will go to that floor now."

So down we went, at about 9 p.m. I grabbed as many books as I could hold.

Unfortunately, our next stop was a large, dim room with no place to sit. The only furniture was hard "delivery room" beds—about as comfortable as doctors' examining tables. The room had no other occupants. When I asked for brighter light to read by, I was told I should sleep.

"Ring a buzzer if you need any help," the nurse said breezily.

"Has she ever tried sleeping during labor pains?" I wondered. I might have complained to my obstetrician, except that she had gone to Yugoslavia that week.

With no light to read by, the night dragged on. There was an occasional visit from the nurse. Mostly, though, she hung out with a couple of others in a little lounge next door. There was a coffee pot and plenty of light out there. But I guessed that regulations didn't allow me to join the party. By the time Anne was born about 7 a.m. (with adequate attention toward the end, I have to admit, from the staff doctor) I was decidedly grumpy.

"Oh well," I said to Steb when he was allowed to see his new daughter. "At least here it's acceptable to have a girl."

He had another happy thought. "And furthermore, courtesy of National Health, she's free!"

Then, a couple of years later, it was Peter's turn to arrive. I felt like an old hand. We were still living in England. The children and I were vacationing in a lovely rented house south of London. Steb commuted to work by train.

There were complications, though. A lot of blood gushed forth one day when the baby wasn't due for 3 months. The doctor said I should stay in bed, preferably in a hospital.

"You really need an ambulance to get there," he said. The village did own one, but it hadn't been used since World War II. That momentous event had ended nine years earlier. However, the ambulance, ancient though it was, did turn up eventually. It managed to transport (I won't say "whisked") me to the Brighton hospital.

The next weeks were exhausting for poor Steb. After work, he had to take the train to Brighton from London to see me. Then he drove to our little town of Henfield. There he read to the children before bedtime, only to perform the same process the next morning. Finally I was declared fit to be moved.

Where to? The Elizabeth Garrett Anderson Maternity Hospital in London. Luckily, we had terrific cook, as well as a nanny, both Hungarian, to look after our house and family.

"How do you suppose I am going to get to London?" I asked a friend who was with me when I heard the news.

"National Health," she responded easily. "We Brits know how to do these things."

She was right. A wonderfully competent nurse accompanied me. Very professional, she supervised my transport from hospital to train. On the train I traveled in a nice, bed-sized compartment. Upon reaching London I was pushed through cavernous Victoria Station on what seemed like a two-wheeled baggage carrier. Then another ambulance and, at last, the hospital itself and a private room.

"No complaint about National Health will ever pass my lips again," I praised.

Peter stayed put almost as long as he was supposed to. Then, as usual, the labor pain department was where the trouble started. This time I was determined not to get stuck for hours on one of those had pallets in the delivery room. Until I deemed the time appropriate, I didn't tell anyone the baby was coming.

That would have worked just fine, except that the elevator didn't.

"Oh dear, the lift has stalled," the morning nurse worried aloud.

By the time a repair man had been found and the elevators were working again, it was too late. My obstetrician, who for once was in the same country as I was, had to deliver the baby in a plain old hospital room.

51

By the time our fourth child was due we were back in the United States. Again I naively stocked up on books to have labor plains by. Once more I arrived at the hospital thinking I knew what was going to happen. Wrong as always.

"We'll just give you something to relax you," said the nurse who showed me to my room.

That suited me. I knew all I needed to know about natural childbirth. What I didn't expect was that I wouldn't surface for 24 hours. By that time Allan had been born and was nicely tucked into a crib beside me.

"What happened?" I asked Steb, who was there with me.

"Modern American medicine," he beamed.

So I saved my paper-back thrillers for a future vacation.

TRAVELING LIGHT
(When Diapers Weren't Disposable)

Reading accounts of parents calmly taking young children around the globe, I tremble with admiration. Steb and I tried it once with a toddler. When it was over we vowed our next travel with children would be when they were in college. The problem was diapers.

After being stationed several years in Beirut, the time had come for two months of U.S. home leave. It began with a leisurely 24-day voyage to the U.S. Jimmy was a year and a half old at the time. A couple of weeks before departure I began to panic. How could we wash and dry diapers for all that time in a small ship stateroom?

Jimmy and I had been casual about toilet training up to that point. Now, after a two-day crash course, it was clear he was not yet ready to change his life style. I started searching for an alternative. One of the embassy wives had arrived recently with a youngster of similar age.

"How did you manage the trip?" I begged to know.

"Nothing to it," she said calmly. "Just use those plastic diaper covers with inserts you can flush away. It's easy."

Plastic diaper covers? Inserts? I had never heard of such miracles. Nobody in Beirut had. You couldn't even buy toothpaste there in 1951.

"I'll tell you what. Since Patty is now trained, you take my extra diaper covers for your trip," she offered. "I'm afraid the inserts are all finished, though."

This was luck. All I had to do was invent the stuffing. Surely that wouldn't be half the strain of living in a stateroom/laundry for 24 days.

Naturally I started with absorbent cotton. It was the most plentiful drugstore item in the Middle East. Cotton fields flourished in Syria and

Lebanon, and apparently took little processing to appear in a box. On trial, however, it didn't work. Half an hour of Jimmy's peregrinations had the cotton hopelessly wadded where it would do the least good. Empty spaces were in all the important spots.

Tissues maybe? Another flop. With enough thickness to be really useful, Jimmy's size increased until I couldn't get him into his clothes.

Finally I found the best material: sanitary napkins. Strategically placed and split in half, three would do nicely. Say six changes a day for 24 days—good heavens, that made 144 boxes!

As an American product, sanitary napkins weren't easy to find. The only prospect was the campus store at the American University of Beirut. There, though the students were Arabs, a number of Americans were on the faculty. They were enough to make importing a few items worthwhile. I tried the store.

"Do you have American sanitary napkins, please?" I ventured to the solitary young man behind the counter. He nodded yes, so I took the plunge. "I'll take thirty-six boxes."

"Thirty-six!" Arabs are supposed to be inscrutable, but this one looked astounded. Apparently concluding I had some extraordinary disease, he brought load after load from the back room. They piled high on the counter.

"Could I have a couple of cartons to put them in, please?"

It should be easy, I thought, to drag the cartons over campus sidewalks to the car, parked some distance away at the college gate.

"Oh, no, madame," I was told firmly. "We must keep all our cartons. We never give away cartons."

Nor did they give away wrapping paper or bags, I found. Customers took purchases as they were, glad enough to find them at all. I slid a large pile of boxes off the counter and started for the door. The young man must have thought I had recovered from my disease, because he made no move to help.

My erratic journey across the campus was highly embarrassing, both to me and to the student body. Strolling couples or groups of students would get within reading distance of my boxes. Then the young people would turn abruptly and head in another direction.

This was an extremely modest country. Women only a few miles away were still wearing bulky garments that covered them from neck to toe, too shy to expose more than their hands and heads. Though half Christian and half Moslem, the custom prevailed in most villages. Such a personal item as I was carrying had to be avoided totally.

I tottered across in stages. One 18-foot box lot was put down on the lawn while I went back for the second. Occasionally a box would topple off the stack or I would graze a branch. Then the whole cargo would tumble down. It took quite a while. Though the campus was a busy one, at no time did anyone venture with in fifty yards of me.

I had borrowed the use of a "company car" for the afternoon. Its driver saw me when I reached the gate. Imperturbably, he took boxes from me. And more boxes.

"Let's just put them in the back seat," I suggested. He began to look somewhat glazed as the stacks grew until there was hardly room for me.

"Oh, that's all right," I soothed. "They're for Jimmy." At that he looked even more glazed.

Well, we got them to the ship all right. Our cabin was crowded for a while but gradually cleared. Jimmy cooperatively used the last of the boxes as we reached New York.

Home leave was wonderful. While there, however, Steb's company transferred him to London. This time the trip seemed too simple to be true. We could fly across the Atlantic in a day. Our luggage would follow by sea in a week.

I was expecting another baby. Several charming maternity outfits were packed in my trunk. They were prettier than my other dresses, I thought. I pictured myself looking very smart at the hotel where we would stay until we found a house.

The flying part was short enough. We got to our London hotel that same night. There we turned on the news broadcast.

"A longshoremen's strike has hit the docks of New York," we heard. "Cargo is piling up fast."

Our luggage, naturally, was part of that pile. It remained so for the four everlasting months of the strike. I alternated between wearing my one frumpy maternity dress and my one baggy suit, letting out seams every two weeks.

Steb and Jimmy were in decent shape with just the clothes carried in their airplane suitcases. But not me. I had brought a big suitcase too, so why didn't I have more clothes?

Taking no chances, I had filled my luggage with disposable diapers.

IN LONDON, IN A FOG

If the Romans were so smart, why did they build the city of Londinium on the foggiest spot in England? And if the Brits are so smart, why did they leave the city there? After experiencing THE FOG of 1952, we Stebingers know why so many centuries were called the Dark Ages. They were really dark from coal smoke.

That historic fog started one Friday during our first December there. Londoners called those thick fogs "pea-soupers."

London at that time held some nine million chilly people. All were housed in buildings lower than nine stories, each structure wearing at least a half dozen chimneys. Those chimneys, for their part, vented smoldering coal fires from millions of rooms.

"It's a temperature inversion," a neighbor explained to us calmly that first day. "Take a giant bowl and place it upside down over the city and you'll get a good picture of our situation. Outside the bowl, the sun is probably shining."

Yes, and it's the place we were told we didn't need a refrigerator because the air stayed so cool. Nor did we need central heat because the air stayed so warm. We and London weather were in a state of serious confusion.

On that Friday it got yellower and yellower through the day. By afternoon we watched men with big flashlights walking the road. Buses followed the men, making their way back to garages. So much for public transport.

By Saturday it was so murky inside our house we could taste the air we breathed. We had to turn all lights on. Each lamp's rays made a distinct outline from shade to floor. Outside was like late twilight from morning on, with complete darkness by two p.m.

The phone kept ringing. "Hello," Steb or I would say.

"Hi, this is Ron Humber across the street. I'm just checking to see if your house is still there."

"Still standing, but probably dissolving fast," was Steb's discouraged reply. Then another ting-a-ling.

"This is Howard," came the voice of an American friend. "I've got claustrophobia. I'm calling to see if somebody is still alive or if I'm the only one left."

Our household made plenty of racket, with all of us coughing. Three-year-old Jimmy, who had asthma, was wheezing loudly. Only Anne, aged eight months, gurgled as usual.

Sunday morning Steb and I decided Jimmy needed to get out to the country to some fresh air.

"I'll stay home with Anne," our nanny offered. She was sure we were insane, which of course we were.

For obvious reasons, there was almost no traffic. The dim daylight was enough to keep us on our way as long as we were on a straight road. Unfortunately, London is full of strange intersections. Five or six roads come together in a circle. At each of these I would have to scout around on foot to get us across. Even then we got onto the wrong road several times.

Have you ever completely lost your sense of direction? We did. It was eerie.

"Isn't fog supposed to stay still?" I asked Steb. "This stuff keeps swirling."

Looking out the windshield, we could see nothing but an eddying wall.

After three interminable hours we were out in bright sunshine at a friend's house. Usually it was not more than half an hour's drive from ours. Jimmy happily played in their garden. We adults enjoyed just looking at each other without peering through muck.

Starting for home again at 4 p.m., we chose a highway with huge floodlights. They were meant to illuminate us most of our way home. Even there, fog was so thick it seemed solid. The lights from above didn't penetrate at all. Neither, of course, did our headlights. I tried walking ahead to guide the car while I shone a lantern at the curb. That was too dangerous, though. Steb couldn't see past the hood.

We settled on a system whereby I hung out the door and shone my lantern at the curb, yelling directions to Steb. He kept veering into the center of the road in the whirl of fog.

"We've lost the curb," I would howl, and he would inch back until we found it again--usually by hitting the darn thing. The worst menace was parked cars that had been simply left on the road. Murder was in our hearts. Then it occurred to us we might well have to leave our own car the same way pretty soon. Jimmy, meanwhile, was perkily singing nursery rhymes in the back seat.

Our hope now was to reach the home of our friends, the Pierces. They lived near the end of a subway line. I still can't fathom how, but we found it. Getting there was a huge relief. I wouldn't have minded being invited to spend the night. However, the English didn't take these fogs as seriously as we did.

"I'll guide you to the underground," Jack Pierce offered.

Carrying a strong light, he beamed it onto brick walls, store fronts, or whatever might appear. When there was a curb to step down or up, he called out to warn us. We all held hands tightly, and Steb carried Jimmy. That youngster felt royally entertained on his father's shoulders.

Occasionally one of us would bump something and bellow, "There's a house on the wrong side of the walk!" only to find we had all crossed a main street without even noticing.

Somehow we ended at the subway station. We couldn't believe how clear the air was below the surface. Apparently, the London underground had to be dug far, far under the soft earth. Down there even fog couldn't penetrate.

Well, we got home, taking 5 l/2 hours for a 50-minute drive. The fog lasted until Tuesday. That made it a full five days, but Jimmy's few hours of fresh air kept him breathing quite nicely. And still singing.

He was in far better shape than the house, which was a study in soot. Sitting on any piece of furniture meant getting up with black spots on clothes where chair or sofa had touched. Sidewalks carried a half-inch of grime.

Worst by far was the death toll. The lungs of 6,000 people in London had simply not been able to survive such filthy air for so long a time. With that, the message finally got through. The city had been warned for years, maybe centuries, that it could not tolerate the use of open fires for heat. Finally they were banned.

Twenty years later our family revisited the scene. Driving into London from the airport, Steb and I were astonished.

"What's happened?" he exclaimed, unbelieving. "Has somebody come and sandblasted the whole place?"

"The buildings are so bright. Give me dark glasses!" I echoed.

The children, of course, were unimpressed.

"Guidebooks say it's a beautiful city," they insisted, "and the buildings are mostly a pretty, soft-colored sandstone."

Sure enough, a whole layer had been cleaned off all urban structures once the fires had been banned. They looked beautiful. I felt as ancient as a Roman soldier.

"You should have seen it in our day, so you would be able to appreciate it now," I said. But as usual, the children had no interest in their parents' olden days.

"First," they planned, "we have to check out the Beatles' studio, and then......."

THE CORONATION OF QUEEN ELIZABETH
or
A CROWNING FOR HER---A BATTERING FOR ME

Yes, it was wonderful to be in London in June of 1953 for the new queen's coronation. No, it wasn't an experience I'd want to have twice. Our house was located near the parade route, which produced complications.

For one thing, we had never known we had so many friends strewn around the world. Letter after letter, phone call after phone call, brought a plea from someone on one continent or another, begging for a place to sleep the night before the event. All over Europe, particularly, excitement before the coronation rose to intensity. Newspapers and television daily showed the arrival of glamorous guests from throughout the planet. Half the world had attempted to get tickets for the show, though few beyond visiting royalty could be accommodated at the ceremony in Westminster Abbey itself. The procession to follow, however, attracted hordes. Hotels, naturally, were crammed far out into the suburbs.

I asked a neighbor why walls were being built along the streets.

"It's to seal off the parade route," she explained, a knowledgeable Londoner.

The route of the coronation parade was strictly walled off, all three or four miles of it. Every open space and sidewalk along the way held bleachers several rows high with numbered seats. Unless one had a ticket for a seat, there was no admission inside the walls. Gates were guarded as fiercely as the crown jewels.

"At least our new house is near Hyde Park and is an easy walk from one of the gates," Steb commented. He had been promoted to manager of the London office and we had inherited an 1820's townhouse in a fashionable section known as Belgravia. Elegant address notwithstanding, the building was an unmanageable six (yes, 6) stories high. Obviously, it was roomy. It also happened that the U.S. businessmen's American Club was in a building on the parade route. There we would be able to watch the ceremony on television in the warm indoors and then move out to a balcony to watch the procession.

As the coronation date neared, we began hearing from friends and acquaintances.

"We haven't heard from some of these folks in years," I noted.

One couple from Rye, New York had won tickets in a charity raffle. Another, from New Zealand, simply had to be there as a citizen of the British Commonwealth. The French manager of Steb's company would be present, not to mention friends from outlying London suburbs and various other parts of the country.

"We need to get closer to the middle of the city," they all pleaded.

The night before the great event every bed, couch and easy chair in our house was taken. Borrowed cushions and blankets littered the floors. In addition, Steb and I had planned a special party for out-of-town business guests the evening following the coronation.

Actually the night of the big sleepover turned out to be fun. Everyone was in a celebratory mood. A catchy new song, "The Queen of Tonga," written about an enormous Commonwealth dignitary who was expected to fill an entire carriage by herself, was on all lips. A chorus might break out at any moment. The drawback was that newcomers to London bombarded the streets, causing a serious shortage of taxis. That, in turn, meant that our guests arrived at all hours.

"Do you realize it's three a.m.?" I groaned to Steb when all were settled. "And we're all supposed to be at our gates by eight o'clock. That means breakfast for this crowd starting about six."

The special day arrived cold and rainy. In the stands, the audience was shown the ceremony inside Westminster Abbey by means of large TV sets. Out there in the streets, long underwear and umbrellas were decidedly helpful, regardless of this being the month of June.

It turned out to be a very, very long day for the spectators in the bleachers. Assembling august personages in the Abbey took a huge amount of time, not to mention the lengthy intricacies of the ceremony itself. The aftermath must have been equally complicated, though no longer televised. Placing the correct prince, prime minister or earl into an appropriate gold-decked carriage was an endless procedure. Chilled and miserable, thousands longed for something, anything, to happen that would relieve the tedium of the interminable wait.

Then, like a thunderbolt from heaven, an announcement came over the loud speakers. A British team had scaled Mount Everest!

Some months earlier, the British expedition had gone to Nepal to try to climb that mighty mountain, which had steadfastly resisted all attempts for centuries. Communication was at an early stage in the fifties, and when the climbing party left its final staging point there could be no continuing reports. Months passed without further word. Fears grew that tragedy had occurred once again. Instead, on this auspicious day came the great news that the group had reached the top. Cheers must have been heard all the way to Scotland.

Eventually, "There they come!" could be heard as the coronation procession emerged. Gilded coaches and carriages were filled with gorgeously-clad, waving royalty and notables. Interspersed were colorful troops from Horse Guards to Ghurkas, accompanied musically by a phenomenal variety of instruments. The time it took for them to pass each person along the way was three hours, and I'll guarantee not one spectator but was riveted to the scene. Magnificence and color actually outdid expectations.

Afterwards, of course, the whole mob headed for the gates at once, so getting home wasn't speedy. Steb and I were both drooping seriously.

"And to think we still have a party to give!" we acknowledged to each other.

Entertaining visitors was part of the job in a foreign post, and London was impossible for any traveler to resist. We had a standard evening program for high-category folks, which we figured the coronation merited. I had duly made necessary arrangements for this very special event.

Our usual drill was to have cocktails and hors d'oeuvres at our house, then head out for dinner and a theater. Sometimes, as in this case, the plan was to dine and dance at a downtown hotel. It should have been easy, but after such an enervating day I was having trouble staying awake.

Things went well enough initially, though dinner service was slow.

"After all, every bite has to honor the new queen," one guest observed.

My eyes stayed open as long as I was engaged in an activity like chewing or dancing. It was when I was supposed to be making conversation that things fell apart. I can't recall ever being so hopelessly sleepy. My mind would simply go blank during a sentence. Climbing Mount Everest seemed comparable.

One time I excused myself, thinking perhaps I could revive by catching five minutes of slumber in the ladies' room, but in the end I didn't dare. I was afraid of staying asleep too long and couldn't take the chance. It helped that I had placed Henri Berard, a French friend who had been one of those using our floor the night before, on my left. We knew each other pretty well, and usually had a good time talking, but tonight one was as exhausted as the other and something had to be done.

"Tell you what," Henri said finally. "I'll talk a while and no one will notice if you close your eyes for a few winks. Then you can give me a turn. It's the only way we can last." Sounds a little crazy, but it worked. Steb's end of the table was just as desperate but they held up too, and at last the day ended.

Queen Elizabeth got through her coronation, and so did we. Barely.

CULTURE SHOCK

How can you have culture shock when you move to your own country? I managed to develop a pretty severe case.

Granted, my first problem when we moved to our new house in Bronxville, New York, wasn't the USA's fault. It was probably mine, though when I avoided the kitchen during my growing up years I didn't see it as serious. After all, my sister Adele liked to cook, and I far preferred to play outside with the rest of the neighborhood kids.

Then, during my first twelve years of marriage, we lived in places where having a cook was the norm. So imagine my shock at suddenly having to produce meals for a husband and four children.

"Luckily," I reasoned, "children under the age of seven won't care what I put in front of them." Wrong.

Hot dogs on Monday, hamburgers Tuesday, fish sticks Wednesday, creamed tuna Thursday, baked chicken parts Friday and spaghetti Saturday worked okay the first week, but weeks two, three and four of the same menu produced minus enthusiasm--carping, actually, and more loudly each week.

And those dishes may sound foolproof, but I found ways to burn even hot dogs.

"You, at least, don't complain," I congratulated Steb. Tactfully, he made no mention of the lunches he ate in the city.

In London, I had been used to having a cook, as well as a nanny for the children and a "daily" to do the cleaning. The dollar paid for a lot in those days.

"Looks like you need a 'mother's helper,' Steb suggested. I followed through promptly.

Our New York suburb had an employment agency which specialized in bringing girls from Britain, and I figured that was just the thing. In short order I was meeting Gloria at the airport.

Gloria's credentials sounded perfect. Aged nineteen, she was the oldest of nine children in a family in Liverpool, all of whom, according to her resume, she had cared for. Our brood would mean less than half as many in her charge. Should be easy.

Gloria was pleasant, but, unfortunately, her sense of responsibility had been left behind in Liverpool.

We vacationed on Nantucket Island that summer, as we would for many years. Though Gloria was helpful at watching over the baby at the beach, I spent my time having to watch over *her.* The U.S. Coast Guard manned the lighthouse near our cottage, and their staff was promptly discovered by Gloria and a friend. Soon I was getting calls from the Coast Guard Patrol to come pick up the girls or they would be arrested. The men were not allowed visitors while on duty in the lighthouse.

"Dating is fine, but being in the lighthouse after hours is not," I said to Gloria. "Why do you keep going there?"

"Because that's the only place there are boys," was the reply.

It's lucky we only rented our cottage for a month because I was starting to lose my enthusiasm for producing bail money.

Back home again, the problem was different.

"Where can Gloria be?" Steb and I wondered when we returned from a cocktail party at nine o'clock one summer evening. Three of the children were still playing outside and it was past everyone's bedtime.

But the only bedtime had been Gloria's. She was fast asleep in her room and claimed the next morning that it wasn't her fault because, "I was tired."

She and I decided to part company so she went to an agency in New York City.

"Guess what!" she exclaimed triumphantly on returning. "I've got a job being nanny to Anthony Bower's two children. Mrs. Bower *loved* my British accent."

Anthony Bower was already a nationally known singer, so the couple must have had a busy schedule. I wondered what I should say about Gloria when Mrs. Bower called me for a reference. Certainly I wished Gloria well, but could never recommend her being in full charge of young children. The call never came, though. I hope her accent was enough for the Bowers to feel secure about the children in her care.

Life improved when I found a mother's helper from West Virginia. Nancy, who was wonderful, lived with us until Allan started school.

Having Nancy there opened a new vista for me. I decided to take a day off every Wednesday.

"Will I be deserting my family if I disappear for a day?" I asked Steb. "And what will I do with all that time?"

"See New York," he urged. "Here's the chance of a lifetime!"

As a semi-New Yorker, having spent some formative years there, Steb was clearly an enthusiast. I, however, brought up in the badlands and plains of North Dakota and Montana, was strictly country.

What do you guess turned out to be the connection between myself and our new city?

Yankee baseball.

In my home town, tiny Rhame, few stations were available on our radios. One of them was in Yankton, South Dakota, with broadcasts reaching out to a huge, sparsely populated area. Of all things, its most popular program was the Yankees. Each afternoon during the season, every store in town had that ballgame on, and ranchers who came to buy hardware or groceries stopped to listen. As had I.

My first day off from Bronxville I went to a game, and thereafter my pattern was: 1) drive to the Bronx and park next to the stadium gate, ready for a quick getaway for home after the last inning, 2) take a subway to the Metropolitan Museum of Art (suggested donation: one dollar. How cheap can entertainment get?), 3) gourmet lunch (still cheap) at the museum café, 4) back to the stadium for my date with Mickey Mantle and Whitey Ford.

Did anyone else in Bronxville attend baseball games on Wednesdays? Not that I ever discovered.

My fellow townspeople, particularly the women I met at PTA and League of Women Voter meetings, spoke English, all right, but it was a different language.

"I'm such a hick," I agonized to Steb. "Every women I like has gone to Vassar or Mt. Holyoke or Wellesley. How do I ever connect with such intellectuals?"

Steb, graduate of an Ivy League college himself, could afford to be calm.

"There's no problem," he comforted. "Those people aren't really snobs. I'll bet you will be great friends some day."

"I'll probably be senile by that time."

I had other things to learn too, it turned out. The children wouldn't fit in if they didn't go to Miss Covington's Dancing School. So I'll be darned if I didn't find myself being an occasional hostess. Each child, in turn, donned the requisite blue suit (boys), bouffant dress (Anne) and white gloves (all) and learned correct ballroom procedure. No one in Rhame would have recognized me.

We lived happily in Bronxville for sixteen years. Those worldly women gradually became my pals, and I got to know New York beyond museums and ball games. I even learned to enjoy cooking. The mighty waves of culture shock gradually smoothed into placid waters.

ADVICE FROM A CAMPING COOK: CONSIDER STAYING HOME

Living only four miles from the New York City boundary has its good points, but privacy isn't one of them. So how does a family get away from the mobs once in a while? Camping was our solution, but that too has hazards, such as starvation.

"I don't want a birthday party," Jim announced at age ten. "I want Dad to take me camping."

Steb was so flattered he dashed out, bought a tent, and off they went. I noticed, though, that the next time the lure came, they asked the rest of us to come too, especially a cook.

This led to lots of family weekends, and we grew to love the sound of bacon sizzling over a morning campfire. In the evenings, pinecones crackled under the pan. All that fresh air surely stimulated appetites, though. Our car, loaded with outdoor sustenance, rode closer to the ground every month as children grew.

For his tenth birthday, Peter chose a visit to a State Park in western New Jersey with a lovely waterfall. As it was late in the year, we rented a cabin with four bunks for the children. Steb and I had a snug tent, so opted for the outdoors. The initial evening meal by a log fire was delightful, and we woke in the morning ready for a big breakfast.

A light snow was on the ground. No problem there, but why could we find so little food to cook?

"We wanted to catch a raccoon for Peter's birthday," confessed our solemn quartet of kids.

"And how would you do that?" we parents asked suspiciously.

"The bathroom has a door to the outside," they explained. "We made a trail of food from the forest to the door, with more inside. Then we

70

took turns going out to slam the door, in case a raccoon had gone into the bathroom."

Sure enough, tracks in the snow looked as if the British Army had passed by. Obviously the children had made an enormous number of trips, and our puny stock of food showed how often the bait had been replenished. Gone were dreams of a campfire breakfast, not to mention a woodsy lunch.

"Oh well, there'll surely be a town with a diner somewhere," I thought.

Indeed, one was. A hike would have to wait until later.

The next birthday it was Allan's turn to pick a place, and he invited the family, plus a friend, to camp in the Catskill Mountains, where he wanted to climb Hunter Mountain, its highest peak. That meant one more mouth to feed, but it was fun. We duly started up the mountain after a good night's rest in our sturdy tents.

At that time, in the sixties, most people had not yet become concerned about a clean environment.

"We don't need our trail map," observed Steb. "All we have to do is follow the beer cans to the top."

The kids, all Scouts at some level, were indignant.

"Let's pick up these cans," they determined, and the next thing I knew they had eaten their lunches to make room in their packs for cans. Naturally, by the time we reached the top they were hungry again, with nothing on hand but empty beer containers.

Anne's idea at that age was to have as her career playing first base for the New York Yankees, so her ten-year birthday party took place in Yankee Stadium with her girls' ball team. That suited me. Plenty of hot dogs and Coke were for sale. This time, however, there wasn't a shortage but too much.

One of the girls, more uninhibited than most, found a fly at the bottom of her Coke cup.

71

"Hey, Mr. Salesman," she yelled. "Bring me a replacement!"

He did so, and she drank with enthusiasm. Then she had a brilliant thought.

"Wow!" she exclaimed. "Maybe I'll find a *cockroach* at the bottom of this one. Then I'll get *two* replacements!"

"Don't these kids," I thought, "*ever* get full?"

Some years went by, during which we found lots of delightful spots to explore. Then, when Jim was about to head for college, we decided on a two-week canoe trip in the Canadian wilderness. With their ages at 12-14-16-18, it sounded very good but, gastronomically speaking, I should have known better.

The best thing was that cans of food would be too heavy, so we were taking dehydrated food, a phenomenal invention. Dishes came with alluring names like Boeuf Bourguignon and Turkey Tetrazzini. We were simply to add boiling water and wouldn't know if we were in the wilds or the Waldorf, except for the taste of mosquito lotion. The big challenge was finding a substitute for bread, knowing well the need for a vast supply of something filling.

I ended up having to rely on numberless packages of tooth-breakers known as "pilot biscuits." These were filling enough but otherwise awful. Cardboard was tastier, and they were exceedingly tough.

Anyway, I bought a mountain of food, and we pushed our canoes off the dock so low in the water that I wondered about our safety.

But not for long. The pile of victuals decreased alarmingly each day. I had bought at least double the recommended amount for every meal. Even so it appeared as though I had deliberately planned to starve the kids into skeletons. Each time we ate I had to deal out rations like a master sergeant or a "tuna salad for four" would quickly become a mere snack for one.

Another thing was the way they *talked* about food. Surely the Canadian lakes we were canoeing through were the most heavenly one could find. Tree-studded islands on bright blue water, so pure you could put a cup into it for a drink any time. Pink granite outcrops sloping into the streams. Loons at dusk giving their mournful cry. But what would we hear by way of discussion? Passionate arguments on the precise texture of a MacDonald's hamburger and (interminably) the exact ingredients of a concoction in our local ice cream parlor known as a "Kitchen Sink."

One day we met a couple who had seen bears and who told us to be very careful in disposing of our leftovers so the smell wouldn't attract bears to our camp. Leftovers! What a hope! Loud laughter from our canoes drifted over the lake as they paddled away.

Of course campers are supposed to eat fish to supplement their diet, but fishing required bait, and anything tempting enough for a fish, believe me, was tempting enough for a teenager. The fish did teach Allan to dive though. He had always steadfastly refused to learn, so we cheered as we spotted him diving off a rock over and over.

"I had to," he panted, clambering up for the last time. "Ten lifesavers dropped off that rock. I HAD to get them before the fish did."

Finally it was the last night. Steb and I sat on one of the smooth granite ledges watching firs darken against the sunset. Loons dived and reappeared across the wind-ruffled water.

"I wonder where the kids are," I mused. "Surely they don't want to miss a minute of this last lovely evening."

The boys, however, were in a tent. I walked over and found them playing poker, of all things.

"How can you possibly waste your time playing poker when…" I started, and then realized it was hopeless. What were they using for poker chips but the last of the rock-hard, tasteless pilot biscuits! Four pairs of eyes gazed greedily at the pot.

I turned away, defeated. If their idea of happiness was to be winner so they could eat the pot when it consisted of *pilot biscuits*, the absolute bottom of the culinary pile, what was an adult with a normal appetite to say?

Those children now tramp the woods with their own progeny. I don't inquire too closely into their camping trips, though. What if they should ask me to come along and cook?

BLACKED OUT IN NEW YORK

"Oh, no! The baby-sitter just cancelled," I groaned to whichever child was near me as I hung up the phone. "It's already five o'clock and I'm supposed to be meeting Dad in New York City at six. What are we going to do?"

"Don't worry, Mom," chirped the optimist beside me. "Us kids can take care of ourselves."

I didn't for a moment trust the gleam in that young eye. Still, it could have been worse. Jim, who had just turned fifteen, was a dependable youngster and the others looked up to him. Anne was twelve, which made Peter ten and Allan eight, all in pretty decent stages, as these things go. Jim shouldn't have to break up too many fights.

When asked, he seemed pleased to take on the responsibility. I decided not to worry whether television might outrank homework this one evening.

"It's a school night, so be sure everyone gets to bed early," I admonished as I went out the door, little expecting anything unusual to disturb normal routine.

But suddenly, as I drove down Manhattan's West Side Highway, I realized something had changed. Lights were still aglow on the New Jersey side of the Hudson River to my right, but on my left all was darkness.

Turning on the radio, I heard a very confounded newsman.

"Nobody knows why the electricity has failed, but it seems to be a big one," he reported. "All of Manhattan and the Bronx are blacked out. Looks like Westchester and parts of Connecticut have been hit, too."

Steb and I had tickets to an event at Madison Square Garden, then located at Eighth Avenue and 32nd Street. Not sure where we wanted to have dinner, we had agreed that I would drive to the Garden and park on Eighth Avenue. There Steb would meet me at six o'clock, having walked there from his office.

When it came time to turn off the highway and onto city streets, I felt the impact. How black it was! My headlights seemed to shine into a void. And I had several large streets to cross. In those first minutes, traffic moved with extreme caution. Cars waited politely for one another at each intersection. We all inched along until I reached the Garden.

There I pulled alongside the curb, locked the doors, and waited in the car. It was hardly a savory neighborhood in which to sit, but there was no way to reach Steb. (A cell phone would have been great, but this was November of 1965, so there would be a wait.) I knew I needed to be where he expected me.

When he arrived at last, I learned he'd had a pretty perilous journey. It started at his office on the 52nd floor of the Mobil skyscraper at Lexington Avenue and 42nd Street.

"There were banks of elevators but only one stairway," he explained. "Luckily, I hadn't boarded an elevator, or I'd still be stuck in there. Dozens of us headed for the stairway. It was pretty narrow, and we had to merge with the crowd already coming down from the floors above. Everyone had to be really careful not to shove. In the pitch blackness, it would have been easy to panic.

"Cigarette lighters weren't much help. What worked was for the person who was nearest the stair rail to hold on with one hand. With the other he grasped the arm of whoever was at his side. A third person did the same on the other side of the stairway. The one in the middle just had to hope they both held steady. The mob moved as slowly as mud.

"We kept talking to stay in touch with those in front and behind us. When somebody stumbled, which inevitably happened, it was really scary."

"Didn't your feet begin to get shaky after a while?" I asked.

"We hardly knew where our feet were after twenty stories or so. From then on they were just numb."

"Finally on the street," he continued, "everyone was disoriented. Buildings were unfamiliar in the blackness. It took a while for me to sort out which direction I should take. I knew I wanted to head west, but where the heck was west?"

Crossing intersections was even harder for pedestrians than drivers. Safety came, of all things, from the universal male urge to direct traffic. Here was their chance! It worked pretty well, too. Amateur "cops" took over. Cars were stopped somehow, while walkers took a turn, then cars again. There were no reports afterwards that any of these good Samaritans had gotten killed, a major miracle.

With Steb finally in the car I proposed we head straight for home. But as I started the engine, someone knocked on the window.

"Can you give me a ride?" panted a woman who sounded as if she had walked all the way from Wall Street. "I'm trying to get to Washington Heights."

"Sure, hop in," I said. "We're heading in that direction."

"I tried to get something to eat," she recalled, settling down, "so I stopped at a deli lit with some candles. A roast beef sandwich was what I ordered, but without their slicing machine they couldn't make it. They were sold out of chicken salad and anything else that didn't need slicing. I settled for just the bread and a hunk of salami that had already been cut. They said they didn't even keep knives on hand anymore. But forget it, sitting down is all I care about right now."

Within the block we had two more hitchhikers, one heading for Harlem, the other for Riverdale, and we managed to squeeze in another at the next intersection. I had never felt so popular.

Our group consensus was that we should head out on Broadway, so I did, only to hit a hopeless jam at Columbus Circle.

"Let me take care of this," offered our Harlem passenger.

He jumped out and somehow maneuvered us through the tangle of traffic.

"How did you do it?" the rest of us asked unbelievingly as he climbed back in on the other side of the circle.

"Military police, Korean war," was the nonchalant response.

Even though traffic was close to impossible, everyone in Manhattan seemed to regard the situation as a big party. People had never behaved so nicely to each other, though many were reeling with exhaustion. Our car was always packed.

Eventually, after saying goodbye to our large number of newfound friends, we reached Riverdale and raced for home on the parkway. By this time it was at least 10:30. Steb and I were starving as well as concerned about how the children had managed to cope with the blackout in Bronxville.

They were all still awake. The house was dark except for the kitchen, but that was lit like a cathedral. I had no idea the house held so many candles. They must have found the Christmas box.

"Since we couldn't turn on the TV, Jim said we had to do our homework," Peter divulged.

"And after that, we just ate," reported Anne.

"I gave you dinner before I left," I protested, but I knew that wouldn't matter. At any moment in time, the four of them could empty a giant refrigerator in minutes.

"Yes, and we thought if the blackout went on for a long time, the food in the freezer would melt too, so we better eat all the ice cream."

So Jim had stayed in control. The kids were pleased with themselves and took off for bed, happy with their adventure.

Steb and I foraged for a replacement for that dinner we never got. Then something struck us.

"Did you see what they used for candleholders?" Steb asked.

The children had unscrewed the bulbs from every light fixture and stuck candles in each of them. By this time there was an inch of wax buildup in every one. Would they ever be usable again?

"Never mind," we told each other.

The whole family had not only survived but, surprisingly, enjoyed the experience. Relaxed at last, we prepared to call it a day.

JAVA, AS SEEN FROM A GOLF COURSE

It's not everyone who gets to start her golfing career as a tournament player. I did, and it was enough to make me take up some alternative sport, like flower picking, where nobody asks your score.

My career started with Steb's transfer in 1972 to Indonesia, where we would be living on the island of Java. We were told to be sure to bring golf clubs.

"Half the oil business in Indonesia takes place on the golf course," our advisor said. "And that's where important social contacts are made too."

It sounded very festive and tropical, so I bought some used clubs and even a yellowing copy of a book, *Modern Fundamentals of Golf.* It had been written by some champion back in the 1930s, and was cheap.

With the trauma of getting settled in a country whose language sounded closer to Martian than English, I had not given a thought to developing my game when Steb blithely announced he had signed me up for a tournament.

"I can't," I wailed. "I'll be an embarrassment. My only exercise in weeks has been practicing vowel sounds."

"Never mind. I hear lots of women who played last year were beginners. You'll be fine."

There wasn't much time to practice so I spent the following morning in our garden, going through my golf book's fundamentals. The gardener could hardly be blamed for thinking I was using my clubs to dig a flower bed in the lawn, but I taught him a new English word ("divot"). Since grass grows quickly near the equator, the damage may not have been permanent.

Ready or not, the time came to head for the tournament course. I had to admit it was lovely, with a majestic volcano looming nearby and tall palm trees lining the fairways. Interspersed were vivid tropical plants and softly rustling bamboo.

When I heard my name on the loudspeaker I headed for my assigned tee. There I found two Indonesian women. Both were attractive, with their thick black hair and delicate stature, and decidedly competent-looking. They smiled at me, then drove their balls far, far down towards the green.

With no choice but to follow, I teed up my ball, swung the driver, and was rewarded by having the ball actually go up into the air and come down in fair territory. A modest effort, but going in the right direction.

We trudged down the fairway, where I duly swatted my ball until it arrived at the green and eventually fell into the hole. I was quite pleased at having ended with an eight, only double the par. My companions both had fours. Since I had never dreamed of playing a hole with anyone so talented as to make par, I complimented the woman nearest me for her achievement.

"Pretty good, making a par on the first hole. Keep it up and soon you'll be club champion."

"Oh, I am already," was the response. "Ani (nodding at the other) is runner-up."

Whatever shred of aplomb I had possessed deserted me as I took my second drive under their expert eyes. Out of bounds. Next try: four feet from the tee box. Third stroke: into water hazard on left. The fact that the hazard was actually a lotus pond covered with sublime pink and white blooms didn't help a bit.

I won't torture you with details of that dreadful hole. Every lie of my ball was worse than the one before—in gooey mud by the water or snared by grass like steel wire in the rough. My score was seventeen for a par three. And I had sixteen more holes to go!

My companions, as one excruciating shot followed another, tried to cheer me up.

"Good. You kept your head down that time."

"Nice out," as I flailed out of a sand trap. That was the highest praise I was likely to hear.

By the third hole we were friends and by the eighteenth I might actually have been enjoying myself if I hadn't known there would be another round tomorrow. Maybe I would get lucky and the night would bring a typhoon or a renewed eruption of Krakatoa volcano.

Later I had the consoling thought that perhaps nobody would know my score anyway. But next morning a monstrous white board had been added to the scene. All the contestants' names were carefully spelled out and ominous boxes beside each name contained yesterday's scores. A quick look showed nobody faintly near my miserable total. Steb's was not too bad. I found him eating a papaya and satay snack as calmly as though the world weren't about to fall in.

"I have just disgraced the family name," I whispered. "We may have to leave the country under an alias."

"Now, now. Our reputation doesn't depend on your golf score. I'm proud of you for trying."

I kept going. My new companions were pleasant, as Indonesians almost invariably are, and played as effortlessly as the earlier pair. Thanks to yesterday's practice my golf had improved to somewhere between bad and horrible. I was beginning to think I might escape without too many double-digit scores, say half.

Then on the seventh hole, after I had churned out of a bunker, my scorer said, "I'm afraid you grounded your club there. That's a two-stroke penalty, you know."

Grounded? Since I had needed three swings to get out, I had naturally taken a bit of sandy ground too, but what could be wrong with that?

The scorer whipped out a copy of *The Rules of Golf*.

See, here in Rule Three: 'When a ball lies in a hazard, the player shall not touch the ground with a club or otherwise before making a stroke.' It's very clear."

I thought it was rotten, myself. What a trick to play on some poor soul stuck in a sand trap. I began to get nervous again, and hit a couple of palm trees. When my ball went out of bounds I glowered at the brilliant hibiscus, waxy frangipani and masses of wild orchids. Gorgeous or not, they were the enemy.

Seeing my ignorance, my new friend the scorer started giving me hints as we walked along.

"Be sure to ask that all opponents' balls be removed from the green when you are putting," she counseled. "If you touch one of them it's two strokes."

I hated to think what other rules might be hiding in that little book.

Finally we holed out on the last green and I walked despondently toward a tropical fruit stand. Stopping by the hateful board, I looked over the rows of numbers. Then suddenly one total stood out from the rest—a score so high, so much worse than the others, even mine, that for a moment I thought they might have put several together by mistake.

It was in the men's column, and was surely the worst total in the tournament's history. The man must have dumped balls in every lotus pond, landed in every sand trap and been out of grounds more than in. My own ghastly effort rivaled Nicklaus by comparison. Indonesian names have lots of syllables, so I couldn't pronounce his, but he was my hero. With that unbelievable score on the same board, no one would waste a passing glance on mine.

Humming, I entered the clubhouse. Maybe life in Java was going to be okay, after all.

MY FLING WITH MING

"Museum?" Steb asked me, amazed. "How could you possibly know enough to work in the Indonesian National Museum when you've only lived in the country two weeks?"

"They do seem desperate," I acknowledged. "I think I was accepted as a volunteer because I can speak English."

I had never thought of that as a particular skill before.

"Besides," I added. "I feel lucky. From the start, I've said I wanted to spend my time in the Far East learning about not only Asian thinking, but also Asian china, and that's what my section will be."

Luck it was. The Indonesian Museum had a fabulous china collection, but the country had been under the rule of the Netherlands for close to four centuries. All labels and card catalogs were in Dutch. Obviously, after Indonesian independence, they needed to be translated into the Indonesian language. In 1972, French and Japanese probably outnumbered English speakers living in Indonesia; nevertheless, it had also been decided to put museum records into English instead of either of those tongues.

I was hooked on ceramics after the first day. Normally a volunteer would never be allowed to touch one of those immensely valuable plates or vases. To write a thorough description of each of them in Dutch, Indonesian and English, though, required our three-person committee to examine each piece in detail. How else to translate and so describe minutely the clay, glaze, slip, footrim, shoulder treatment, patterns and so on?

"I'm in love with every dish," I confided to Steb. "I even dream of them!"

"At least you're enjoying it," he was glad to hear. "Are your fellow volunteers equally nutty about the stuff?"

"Yes," I acknowledged. "They may dream in languages of Indonesian or Dutch, but the colors in all our visions are the same—celadon or blue and white."

Once caught, the disease stayed with me. There were constant reminders. The Java Sea is dotted with small islands, lovely for swimming and snorkeling. Through the clear water one often saw colorful broken pieces of ancient china in the shifting sands, relics of long ago shipwrecks or trading posts.

Door-to-door salesmen, called "tukangs", were also numerous.

"Can you believe they carry these antique dishes on bicycles and motorcycles?" I exclaimed incredulously to our son Allan (still in high school, therefore living at home. The other three children were in college in United States, half a world away.)

"One was here this afternoon with no fewer than forty specimens hanging from his motorcycle. He kept bringing them out of saddlebags and pockets until they covered the porch!"

Much bargaining would ensue, at the measured pace which was the custom in Java. Not a great deal of my money was spent, however, since the items tukangs could carry were fairly small.

When examining my purchases at leisure, I usually found chips and cracks that had been painstakingly and skillfully disguised. Then one day an uncommonly complete small jar appeared. Its color was a deep blue and the pattern just right. I thought I had found a bargain.

Soon after, some folks came to our house for dinner.

"You know this is a fake, don't you?" asked a knowledgeable friend as he picked my prize off the coffee table.

"Oh, sure," I lied. "But has can you tell, exactly?"

I thought I had learned a few things from my museum mornings, but apparently had far to go.

"See the glaze," he responded. "It's been sandpapered to make it look old. And those ears," pointing disdainfully to its small handles. "They would never have been attached that way."

He went on to explain that a flourishing ceramics industry had recently sprung up in Thailand, where they were copying 13th and 14th century Chinese ceramics.

"They have a pretty blue and white color, and the patterns are authentic, so they appeal to tourists," he continued. "Keep yours and enjoy it."

That's what I did. I still have it and I still love it, but with no illusions.

Gradually I felt secure enough to buy bigger and more expensive china. A friend, Marcy, and I even went on shopping ventures to other Indonesian islands like Bali and Sumatra. The best trip was to an island group that used to be called the Celebes, on the Makassar Strait.

"Watch out for pirates," Steb cautioned me. "Makassar used to be famous for them. Maybe you can find some descendants."

"With my luck, it's practically guaranteed," I sighed. But that didn't make me stay home.

Once there, Marcy and I stayed with Indonesian friends who knew lots of china dealers, with whom shopping was extremely informal. Dealers didn't have stores, but invited us to their homes (some with wood floors, some with dirt, some on stilts). There they nonchalantly pulled ceramics out from under beds and from inside drawers.

One village was down the coast where there once had been a thriving city. Now it was just rice fields and second-growth jungle. We were invited into the house of a man who was called the "head." I thought he was headman of the village but he turned out to be the head digger. He had a number of attractive pieces for sale so we chatted a while. Then suddenly he jumped up and said, "Come see."

Accompanied by villagers, off we went across rice paddies, slipping and sliding in the mud, often up to our knees in water. On arrival at a grove of large trees, we were surprised to see bits of broken china. Near them were a number of long brass rods. This was the graveyard, they said, of long-ago ancestors (not necessarily theirs).

"It was good luck to be buried with ceramics from China," one of the men explained. Holding a brass rod, he showed how he would pound it into the ground until it hit a piece of china. That meant he had found a grave.

"Then," he continued, "I dig down twelve or fifteen feet to where the skeleton is."

"But don't you break china that way?" I wanted to know.

"Of course. But it doesn't matter. There's always more."

He flopped on the ground and gave a brisk impersonation of a buried body. His hands pictured a plate over its face, arms around a couple of big vases, an offering dish or two on the chest and stomach, and several rice bowls alongside the legs.

"Those old Chinese must have been terrific salesmen," observed Marcy. Our hosts thought that idea hilarious.

At this stage of the rainy season they couldn't dig. Their holes would be too full of water to get to the required depth. I don't know what the religion of these villagers was (a few miles inland, people believed water buffaloes were sacred) but they said they were considerate of the bones. The china was packed away very carefully, not to disturb any remains.

Marcy and I thought this might be a clandestine operation, but apparently not. It was broad daylight and there was much hello-ing to people we met along the wet paths.

Back in the village, I purchased a couple of Ming dynasty (1350-1650 A.D.) blue and white offering dishes. Marcy bought some Sung dynasty celadon which came from an even earlier period, affirming the graves had been there quite a while.

By the time we Stebingers left Jakarta and moved to Columbia South Carolina, I had a respectable collection, concentrating on Ming blue and white china. In Columbia, I tenderly nursed my Ming babies for over twenty years.

When it came time to move to Connecticut in 1996, though, I couldn't face the hassle of moving those precious pieces of my past. The solution? A gift to the Columbia Museum of Art, which accepted them happily. Most of the 65-odd pieces had to be stored, but each time I have been back to Columbia, different items from the Stebinger collection were on display in the museum's South Asia section. If you head that way, you are hereby invited to have a look.

HOW TO BOARD A PLANE THROUGH THE FOOD CHUTE

Everybody has a horror story about an airplane trip, so if you think you've heard them all, skip this chapter. On the other hand, if you don't know one that includes the ice storm of the century, a bloody hijacking at the Rome airport, and a family member's arrest as an international spy, read on.

Here's the setting: In 1973, Steb and I were living in Jakarta, Indonesia with youngest son Allan, who was attending high school, while Jim, Anne and Peter were in various American colleges. Naturally we wanted to have Christmas vacation together, and Jim proposed spending it in Nepal, where we could take a trek in the Himalayan mountains.

With enthusiastic acceptance all around, plans were made and we were to meet in Kathmandu, Nepal on December 22. The Jakarta contingent arrived a couple of days early.

"Everything looks good," I reported after calling our outfitter on arrival. "The trek is set up, though our schedule is tight. We have to fly to the Annapurna Mountain area the morning after our college kids arrive. And get this—we'll be met by three Sherpa guides and fifteen porters, with enough food and gear to keep us tented and fed for eleven days."

"Terrific." Allan was game. "How high is Annapurna?"

"Over 26,000 feet," I read from our instructions. "It's not Everest, but almost all the peaks in that region are still up there in the jet stream."

"But we can't climb that high," Allan realized.

"Don't worry. We'll only climb to a place called the Annapurna Sanctuary at 14,000 feet."

The city of Kathmandu appeared to have been frozen in time around 1450. However, there were a few twentieth century touches, including a decent hotel, where we settled down to wait for the rest of the family.

In the meantime, tickets on Air India had been sent to Peter, who was in Boston. He lived closer to the New York airport from which they were to embark than Anne, in San Francisco, or Jim, in Tucson. When the day came, Peter was all set to take a shuttle flight and meet his siblings at Kennedy Airport in New York for takeoff at 7 p.m.

But Nature had other plans. An unexpected ice storm locked Boston in its frozen tentacles. When Peter checked with the airport to learn whether planes were flying, nothing could move from there—not his flight, not any flight.

Rushing to the train station, he managed to crowd onto a coach for New York. However, the usual four-hour trip stretched to more than five. By the time the train reached Penn Station, the clock showed he should already have been at the airport.

Frantically seeking a taxi, he ran to the head of a line.

"This one's mine, kid," snarled the burly businessman who was first, shoving him out of the way. Pleadingly, Peter looked at the taxi driver.

"I HAVEto get to Kennedy Airport," he beseeched.

The driver had been sent from heaven. Recognizing desperation when he saw it, he said, "Sorry, sir," to the man in the queue and took off with Peter through the rush-hour melee.

In the meantime, Jim and Anne were at the airport ready for takeoff, but still without tickets. They waited and waited at the Air India gate, taking turns searching for Peter in case he was somehow in the wrong line. The passengers boarded, the final call for takeoff was announced, and still no Peter.

"Can't you keep the plane open a little longer?" they begged at the desk. Anne, accomplished at shedding an effective tear when needed, managed to promote a few minutes' delay, but even the friendly attendants could not hold an international flight for long. Adding to Jim and Anne's dismay, when asked about the next flight to Kathmandu they were told all flights were sold out until mid-January! The attendants closed the boarding desk, turned out the lights and left.

Despondently, Jim and Anne wandered back towards the main concourse, where they were finally joined by an ashen Peter fully an hour after the plane left the gate. The three of them sat in the echoing airport, dejection in every muscle,.

Suddenly Anne jerked up. One of the public address announcements had a familiar sound.

" Wasn't that the number of our flight?" she asked, with a surge of hope.

Racing to the Air India lobby desk, they heard astonishing news. With the intimidating weather, takeoffs had slowed to a creep. Their plane, still in line, had a late (and obviously important) passenger who was to be driven out to it.

"Can't we go out to the runway too?" they pleaded.

"I suppose you could," admitted the clerk. "You can try to get on, though the plane's doors have closed, so you'll have to go up the food chute. Hurry! I'll hold the station wagon."

They hurried, all right. Their driver maneuvered carefully to the line of planes through heavy sleet. The ground beneath his tires grew more slippery by the minute. That ice storm from Boston was working its frigid way west. Miraculously, the correct plane was located, and, weak with relief, they were soon crawling up the food chute and heading for points east.

Rome, the plane's first stop, was reached the next morning, but not quite as planned. Shortly before landing, an agitated captain's voice came on.

"Folks, it looks like something has happened here. We need to get fuel, so we have to land, but they're telling us to get going again quickly. Sorry you can't get off the plane as expected."

What could it be? As they touched ground, passengers crowded around the windows. Nothing exceptional could be seen except maybe more activity than usual. Then, during refueling, someone came aboard and excitedly recounted events. Dramatic events they were. A gang had suddenly emerged, intending to hijack a Lufthansa plane. There had been resistance from security forces and possibly from some passengers and crew. That had led to a gunfight and at least a dozen deaths before the hijackers managed to commandeer the plane and take off.

Those events had occurred in a different part of the airport, but it was possible more hijackers might still be in the area. Their Air India pilot was in no mood to hang around once he had some fuel, and none of the passengers relished being held for ransom, so off they flew for the next stop, Kuwait.

It wasn't long before the pilot's voice came on again.

"Sorry to have to adjust plans another time, but the hijackers picked Kuwait for their next landing," he reported. "We don't have enough fuel to reach New Delhi, which is on our schedule next. However, the Bombay airport can take us. We'll be landing there."

At last they burst off the crowded plane. Walking around the airport felt good, and would have felt better if Jim hadn't decided he should get rid of some shotgun shells he had noticed in one of the side pockets of his backpack. The shells seemed harmless enough, and certainly had been so in Arizona. There, small game hunting in the desert was part of the lifestyle.

"With the nervous tension in the air around here, I might be searched," he thought. "So why take a chance?" He shook them out into a nearby trash can.

But somebody was watching. An alarm sounded, security guards swarmed around, and he was hauled off for interrogation.

Anne and Peter stood by helplessly. Their plane was due to take off soon. Would their tickets be good on another flight or would they be spending Christmas in Bombay? Worse yet, would their brother languish in an Indian jail for the next few years?

Jim, after being searched vainly for any more lethal possessions, was questioned endlessly about the shotgun shells. No, they couldn't be used to blow up anything without the shotgun itself. No, he wasn't part of a hijacking ring. No, he had no harmful intentions toward Indians or Hindus.

Patiently, he went through the same procedure with three levels of interrogators. None of them seemed to have either much sympathy or much power. Time was slipping by and he didn't want them deciding to put him in jail "just in case." Realizing how edgy they were after the carnage in Rome, he felt more and more defenseless. Finally, someone appeared who seemed to have more authority.

"Look," Jim pleaded. "You can see I'm not part of a gang. You have examined not only me, but every single shotgun shell as well, and all are harmless. Why not let me join my brother and sister and go on to Nepal?"

Still no affirmative response, while his custodians discussed his fate. Eventually, Jim decided to move to a different level.

"I should inform you that my father, who is waiting for us in Kathmandu, is the Vice President of Mobil Oil Indonesia," he told them. "I guarantee that holding me needlessly would bring attention from the American embassy and a major international corporation, maybe even newspaper reporters. Do you want to look foolish for holding an innocent student?"

That did indeed start them thinking. A hurried consultation brought a suggestion for compromise. Would Jim leave India on the next plane and promise not to return? No problem there! He rejoined his hugely relieved siblings and they were on the next plane out of Bombay.

Meanwhile, Steb, Allan and I had gone happily to the airport to meet their flight from New Delhi. We hoped they had had plenty of rest on their trip so they could get up the following morning ready for the plane ride towards Annapurna. Alternative tickets were now nonexistent, like all vacation time travel arrangements. We <u>had</u> to catch that airplane. Their flight came and we watched with growing concern as passengers disembarked, then crew, and no Stebingers. The next flight from India wasn't for four hours, and it was coming from Bombay, not New Delhi.

Pulling the whole vacation together had been my job, and I was beginning to feel some panic.

"I don't think I can handle watching passengers file off another plane," I agonized.

It happened that Steb and I had been invited to tea with friends of friends who were in Kathmandu, bird watching, of all things. Allan offered to continue to wait at the airport so we could go off to quiet our nerves, if tea would do it. To be honest, Scotch would have sounded better. Our hosts were interesting people, so the time passed pleasantly, though I looked at the phone more than the birds. Finally it rang, with the good news that all was well.

Some time later, Anne told me that the final scene in her mind of that harrowing expedition was our cheerful inquiry at the baggage claim: "I hope you had a pleasant trip!"

AN AMAZING PLACE

Do you think you've heard of most world religions? If so, is the worship of water buffaloes on your list? I don't know what the creed is called, but my encounter with its customs was memorable.

While living in Indonesia, I had the chance to go with a group of women to the interior of the largest island in the Sulawesi island group. Some special funeral rite was to occur in a place called Tanah Toraja. The islanders, wishing to promote tourism, invited us to come.

Getting to Tanah Toraja was no joy ride. Only tough four-wheel-drive vehicles could even attempt to navigate the road. We passengers were tossed on our stiff bench seats like popcorn, wondering what comforts, if any, awaited us at our final destination.

The small guesthouse was fine, though, except that we each had to bring our own sarong to use as a sheet—a common requirement in Indonesia. It was near a village. That afternoon we look a walk, fascinated especially by the strange-looking houses. Instead of roof lines that went down at the eaves, these went up. Also, at the front of each structure, a beam extended straight down from roof the ground. On the beams were fixed a number of upturned objects.

"They could be horns," was one woman's comment. "But whose horns? They're too big to fit onto cattle." Then came a thought. "Do you think these could have anything to do with the water buffaloes they've been mentioning?"

She turned out to be right. They did come from water buffaloes, but not run-of-the-mill ones. Only very special, giant horns earned a berth as house decorations. It was picturesque, though decidedly unusual.

The next morning our driver took us for an outing. Mountain peaks towered overhead. Sheer cliffs formed the lower vistas. The road got ever worse.

"It's no wonder this place is so isolated," was an early remark. "Nobody could have found it before this road was built."

"And when they did get here, how did they live?" came the question. "Surely this rocky ground can't be farmed."

"Hey, look at the cliffs," said another. "There are some odd-looking caves in them. And something is built around the cave entrances. Can they be balconies?"

"Now it's getting really weird," announced a younger woman. "There are people standing on the balconies!"

This was too much. We had the driver stop and tried to get an explanation. Most of us had been taking Indonesian language lessons, and we hung on each word.

"Land which is rich enough to grow food is too precious to use for burials," we interpreted from his rapid explanation. "Holes in the cliff are hollowed out so families can be placed there instead."

"But who is that standing on the balconies? They are all dressed and some even seem to be waving at us."

"Those aren't people. Just life-size dolls that were made in the likeness of those who died."

"They must cram a lot into each tomb," we observed. "Those balconies are full."

There were lots of them, too. Everywhere we looked more tombs appeared, hidden in the canyon walls.

It wasn't long, given the condition of the road, before our shaken bodies were ready to give up the day's sightseeing.

The next day was the funeral our group had been invited to attend. We settled our now-creaky bones back into the vehicle. Luckily, not far beyond yesterday's trip, the valley widened out. Coming over a rise we got a view of a large open area circled by several buildings. People were visible, and a few animals.

Then new clusters of visitors could be seen, arriving not only from the other end of the valley but from passes in the rugged terrain off to each side. Each batch of newcomers had in its midst what could only be a water buffalo. Up closer, the animals looked much like the American buffalos some of us had seen in Yellowstone Park—thick front quarters with leaner hind ends. Unlike the Yellowstone version, though, these bore giant sets of turned-up horns on their heads. No doubt remained as to the origins of the house decorations in the village.

The road ended abruptly. We foreigners were ushered into a bamboo structure. It appeared temporary, with lengths of bamboo in the walls separated by an inch of daylight. All windows and doors were simply openings.

We were greeted enthusiastically and offered something that looked like chopped green leaves. Following our hosts' gestures we each put a handful of it into our mouths. I chewed mine carefully, which took quite a while, gradually beginning to notice that my mouth was becoming numb. At the same time, I was getting rather lightheaded. The proceedings took on a dream-like quality.

Delicious bits of food were served and we were beginning to relax. Then came a commotion at the doorway as a giant water buffalo was led up. It looked benign enough, but what followed wasn't. The man leading the buffalo whipped out a huge knife and swiped it across the beast's throat, severing its jugular vein. Blood gushed, making a large pool, as the critter sank quietly to its knees.

I'm not sure how we would have reacted without the sirih (betel), which is the mild narcotic those green leaves turned out to be. As it was, stunned but docile, we realized we had been given our entertainment for the moment. We and fellow guests were led to the second floor of another of the bamboo structures.

Some of these guests spoke Indonesian.

"Tell us about this place," we begged.

97

It seemed the Tanah Toraja tribe had in ancient times lived on the coast. When invaders came, they retreated farther and farther inland, finally reaching these interior mountains. The clan was safe, but in the rocky terrain they couldn't grow food. They all thought they would die. Then a mysterious hero appeared, leading water buffaloes. The animals produced milk and meat and the people were rescued. No wonder they began to worship their saviors.

"What's happening today?" we asked next.

"We are guests at the funeral of a very important man," they told us. "A water buffalo was killed in our honor."

That was an honor? I hoped never to be so honored again.

"It will be given back to the villagers who brought it with them to the funeral. They will feast on it for days. Others will do the same for additional visitors."

Suddenly a bell rang. Peering down into the fence-enclosed center, I asked again what was going on.

"They are getting ready to take the effigy doll of the deceased for a ride," someone explained. "See the fancy carriages without wheels?"

Searching more closely, I saw a number of brightly-decorated small sedans fitted to wooden axles, and being carried on their shoulders by young men.

"Those will carry effigies of the deceased and others of the family who died earlier."

"Aha! Some of the dolls from the cliffside balconies?" I thought.

"Young men will carry them on their shoulders. Let's go down stairs and get a closer look."

Our whole party, plus other more recently-arrived guests, dashed to the circular parade ground. Players of varied instruments, mostly bamboo pipes and reeds, tootled merrily to an accompaniment of drums, gongs and tinkling metal. They started to march around the large circle.

"Here come the funeral figures," our local acquaintances alerted us.

Four or five "cars" were then carried in with the effigies of the newly-deceased in the one in front. All was merriment. Every little while the young men carrying the sedans stopped and gave their passengers a good bounce, some of them having to be resettled into their places when they fell out.

After half an hour or so the procession left the central circle to wind among visiting villagers, some of whom had set up tents and seemed to plan on staying a while.

"This is a great party. When does the funeral start?" I asked.

"This is it. The man died four years ago."

"Four years! Isn't that kind of a lengthy wait?"

"Not at all. It takes a long time to save the money for an affair like this. The family has to pay the villagers to kill their best water buffalo, even if the locals do get to eat the meat. That's why the family is given the horns of the animals killed here to adorn their house."

I won't say everything eventually fit into place. I will say that we visitors returned to Jakarta with an experience we weren't likely to forget.

HOW (NOT?) TO LOOK FOR A JOB AT AGE 53

With stock market charts sinking off the bottom of the page and college costs sailing over the top, I decided it was time for me to add to the family coffers.

Steb had retired from Mobil. His years in hardship posts let him do so at an early age, and he had taken a position (after considerable searching, I must add) at the University of South Carolina as Distinguished Lecturer in the Masters of International Business (MIBS) program. We planned to start our new careers at the same time.

I had always liked numbers and decided to take the H & R Block tax course and work for them during the tax season. Steb supported the plan. I finished the class and was all set when income tax time came. Like most other preparers, I liked the job.

"It's like a mystery novel," I confided to a fellow worker. "I don't have any idea how the tax return is going to come out until the very end. Do you?"

"Generally a surprise," he agreed. "And it's really nice when the customer doesn't owe anything."

It was true. We hated having to break the news when a sizeable amount appeared on the "tax due" line.

People brought an amazing amount of paper with them. But most of it was just electric bills and various other documents that wouldn't help them any. It sure slowed things down though.

As novices, we weren't given complicated returns, but even then we would complete only a handful in a day.

The "proving out" process was the biggest hurdle. As each return was completed we were to put a series of its numbers into our adding machines. By some magic the total was supposed to come out zero, which would prove our work was correct. If it equaled anything else (which was often) the whole thing had to be done over again.

One tax preparer revealed that he had taken Block's course three times and worked the equivalent number of tax seasons before more than half of his proofs produced that crucial zero on his first try.

Another problem: the office was near an army base and many soldiers needed tax forms filled out for their home states.

"Why can't states all use the same forms?" we complained. "Instead they compete to see which can confuse us the most."

Well, April 15th arrived on schedule, and soon after that we got paid.

"Four hundred dollars!" I complained loudly to Steb that night. "Working on commission for a low-fee company was never expected to put us on easy street, but this will hardly buy dog food."

Maybe I should try for an Administrative Assistant slot, I thought. One was available through an office temporary agency, and I showed up hoping my 30-year-old typing skills hadn't evaporated. After all, I did my own letter writing that way.

The trouble was, electric typewriters had sneaked onto the scene while my mind was on raising children. My own portable typewriter was stiff from a rebuilding job some years earlier and the keys had to be batted with fingers of steel. This time the machine I was given had an electric monster inside which snapped levers up like a machine gun if my fingers so much as hovered over the keys. Each page I copied was rife with errant kkkks and ffffs. A day was all I lasted.

How about teaching, I mused. I did have an ancient Minnesota teaching certificate, the result of some stupefying education courses in college. I had even endured a three-week bout of practice teaching in a hapless small town near the college. After that experience, unfortunately, I had sworn never to be caught anywhere close to a school again.

It wasn't the classes that made a wreck of me, it was the noon hours. Most of the children stayed at school for lunch, and the regular teachers would gaily depart for a hot meal. That left the practice teacher to police corridors full of nameless young faces, each one hiding some fiendish plan to harass me.

"Don't worry about the kids. They'll just eat their sandwiches and go outside to play," the practice teacher before me had pronounced glibly. "All you have to do is see that they don't congregate in the halls."

What she didn't tell me was that the weather forecast was for a cold wave.

When I arrived the temperature was 15 below and just cooling off. (I'm not exaggerating. This was Minnesota in January.) Outside to play? Any student with sense would eat in the furnace room. There, I hoped fervently, they would huddle until class time.

The first day I established myself by the newel post of the main stairs, placed a book on the post and tried to look both fearless and nonchalant. An occasional child flitted by and I tried a benign smile, invariably met with total blankness as though the post were standing there without me. At least there was silence, which I assumed meant I was in control.

Suddenly came a rumble from somewhere above. I looked up to see a wall of faces with no torsos at the top of the steps. The wall came closer. The entire student body, probably a hundred youngsters, was sliding down the stairs headfirst on their stomachs—a great sea of children, all sizes, bumping solemnly downward as though they did it this way all the time.

What would the principal think! Surely this must be "congregating." They thumped to my level and calmly started down the next set of stairs.

"Get up," I said in my firmest tone, a faint squeak. No one paid the least attention. The leaders reached the bottom, marched back up along the steps and promptly started back down again the same way.

This performance actually lasted the whole lunch period and, pillar of jelly that I was, I meekly stood at my post pretending to read, while the children surged up and down like lemmings. My great fear was what the other teachers would say when they came back.

This concern, at least, was groundless. At the sound of the quarter-to-one bell, the sliders quietly disappeared and the adults came back to find an empty hall, empty stairs. Nobody but a weak-in-the-knees practice teacher, still reading the same paragraph.

Can you believe the whole mad procedure continued every day until the cold wave receded? Naturally that didn't occur until my three weeks were almost up.

Well, all that had happened years ago. With the attainment of a master's degree and my present state of maturity I ought to do better. I went to the graduate education section of the university. There the advisor was far from supportive.

"You could get the degree all right," she stated. "But a beginner in her mid-fifties? What school would hire you?"

Deflated, I tried the graduate accounting school. Same discouraging result.

"A woman who is practically at retirement age and with no experience whatever…not a chance," was the glum conclusion.

"Surely there's *something* you can do that's useful," Steb commiserated. Easy for him to say, I thought ungratefully. His own new career was going swimmingly.

The next day my phone rang. The real estate agent who had sold us our house had spotted a help-wanted ad in the newspaper.

"They're looking for a recruiter in a head-hunting agency," she informed me. "It's for somebody who is familiar with the whole country. Heck, you're familiar with practically the whole world."

I applied and was hired, though the pay was entirely commission and I knew I might never make a cent. Anyway, it would be a new experience. Of the ten recruiters in the office, most were men in their twenties and thirties. All were cocky and highly energetic. Phones rang from all directions.

"There's a big demand for engineers and geologists," said my new boss—a thirty-something himself. "We are part of a national corporation, so both jobs and applicants could be anywhere in the country. Companies pay us to find good people for them."

The system was to phone a geologist, say, who had been in our files, and if he already had a good position, to see if he knew anyone else who was looking for a better job in a different location. On the other hand, if I found a good-sounding applicant I would need to find a company which was looking for an employee with the skills he or she had to offer. We rarely met candidates or employers in person, since we were in South Carolina and they might be in Texas or Maine. The work proved stimulating, and I didn't mind being called Mom occasionally. I did bristle when I once heard myself described as the "Office Grandmother."

It took dozens of calls to find a good match, and could be discouraging for lengthy spells. When such a fit finally surfaced, phone interviews and personal interviews had to be set up, plane and hotel reservations made, references checked and...and...and...and. Glitches were constant and competition intense. When a job offer was finally made, hurdles were still high. Salary negotiations could drag on, ruffled feelings had to be soothed, and wives or husbands convinced they really wanted to make the move to some godforsaken place in the Texas Panhandle, say. That meant checking school systems, recreation opportunities, even churches. Try locating a geologist's position with a nearby quilting group for mom, children's ice skating and a Ukrainian Orthodox church. The entire enterprise was a giant jigsaw puzzle.

Amazingly, I found I had a knack for putting situations together.

"All those years refereeing children's neighborhood feuds and interviewing political candidates for the League of Women Voters seem to be of some use after all," I told Steb. "Not to mention having to talk diplomatically to people from England to Indonesia."

After a year or so I dashed home with great news.

"Can you believe this? In the last quarter I was top producer in the office!"

Steb was as stunned as I.

"You mean an old codger like you can outdo all those young dynamos?" he chortled. "At that rate you'll soon be earning more than I do." He seemed to relish that idea.

We poured a drink and pondered.

"I have to admit I'm no smarter or more skilled than they are," I acknowledged. "Sometimes, though, I feel like I have a little more common sense. There's such a thing as understanding real life, and then you can deal with it, not attack it."

"I'm finding my years are no hardship either," agreed Steb. "Maybe all those crises we've lived through helped us learn to cope a little better, even though they were disasters at the time."

"Do you realize what has happened?" I added. "What's helping us now is that very same maturity everybody thought was such a handicap."

A few years later I formed my own company—Nationwide Medical Recruiters—and found it so rewarding I didn't retire until age 74. Steb did even better—he worked to 75.

Whoever would have guessed?

TWENTY YEARS AS PSEUDO-SOUTHERNERS

Imagine a city where spring starts on Washington's birthday and where ravishing blooms like camellias, wisteria and magnolias are flowering year round. Then place it between 7000-foot mountains and sandy ocean shores, people it with southern charmers, and you have Columbia, South Carolina. Once we could decipher the southern accents, it was great.

Tired of so much traveling, Steb had retired from Mobil at age 57. Then he embarked on a second career at the University of South Carolina, while I started a career of my own. With our youngest in college by then, we were free to explore our new world. And, sticking to our lifetime motto that anything worth doing is worth overdoing, we wasted no time.

First, close to home, was the Forest Lake Country Club, with one of its fairways across the street from our new house. Jogging near its fairways in early morning, we were serenaded by astonishing varieties of birdsong. It happens that Columbia is on the northern edge of a southern bird zone and the southern end of a northern one, not to mention its proximity to the Atlantic flyway and exotic habitats like Four Holes Swamp. We became increasingly popular with bird-watching friends from points as far as London.

Our dog, Tessa (a hunting breed) was a bird watcher too, but for different reasons. She learned in a hurry not to challenge the great blue heron that frequented the golf course water hazards, and a mother duck became a problem for her as well. One morning Tessa came upon its nest near a tall oak. The duck promptly waddled toward the lake to distract attention from her eggs, and the dog followed behind, carefully proceeding at waddle pace also, but in excited circles.

I was close by and could read her thoughts: "How is a self-respecting bird dog supposed to point at one that doesn't hide, but just waddles?" Poor Tessa.

Southern history was another lure. One of our best friends was a history professor and we would visit historic places all over the state, learning about bygone days without having to turn a page. Cities like Charleston and Savannah are lovely, but give me a plantation house with its white columns and stately, tree-lined driveway, surrounded by moss-laden oaks. Such mansions would sometimes be watching over a lazy river or up-country vista; others looked out on seaside rice fields and tidal marshes. They seemed arrested in time.

The Carolinas were fully involved in both the Revolutionary War and the Civil War (always called "*The* Woh"), so there was no lack of memorable battle sites from mountains to swamps. Also, 4,000-year- old Indian mounds could be found along the coast. Picture ring-shaped mounds fully ten feet high, big enough to surround a village, the walls consisting entirely of seashells.

I bet it took at least a thousand years just to eat the seafood that was once inside those shells," was Steb's comment.

Friends still owned country plantations and farmhouses handed down from their ancestors, a bit decrepit by now, sometimes, but wonderful for weekends. Another thing about South Carolina is that young people don't want to leave it (not like my North Dakota, alas, though climate may be a factor.) That can make family parties pretty sizeable. I remember one Thanksgiving when Steb and I plus 27 family members, not counting dogs, had Thanksgiving in one of those old farmhouses. Nowhere had we been introduced so frequently to "my third cousin once removed" and similar designations.

"Would you like tickets to the Masters Golf Tournament?" was a question always music to our ears. Prominent local people had been given such tickets from the tourney's earliest days. Interestingly, those folks were never allowed to pass from this earth, at least as far as the ticket list was concerned.

"Pick your day," one of our friends told us. "Those tickets are getting expensive and the family says it's tired of chasing golfers all over the course. Television works much better."

We usually chose the final day. Our system was to follow one pro foursome the entire eighteen holes, thereby fixing the layout in our minds. Then we settled down on a hill by the 17th green with a clear view of both fairway shots and putts. From there we watched the golfers play their last round, leaders coming last, of course.

"What a day!" Steb or I would exclaim happily on return home, too tired even to hang up our sun hats. Part of the Masters scene was the gorgeous display of azaleas, but we could be blasé about that too, our own garden showing the same profusion under its tall pines.

"Tough life," we agreed each spring.

Of course there's another side to the story of weather along that southern coast—hurricanes. Columbia was over a hundred miles inland, so those awful storms were rarely a menace there. We spent dozens of weekends with friends along the coast, however, so felt very concerned about the storms when they threatened.

The worst of the hurricanes during our South Carolina years was "Hugo" in 1989. As it happened, we were far away—on a cruise along with ten other Columbia couples. Where was the cruise? Of all places, the Black Sea and Greek islands of the eastern Mediterranean. Our ship was approaching Crete, as I recall, when the hurricane news arrived. Many of the couples with us owned beach property, so worry was intense. No one wanted to wait until we got home to find out exactly how their cottages had fared.

Remarkably, modern telecommunication was such that there was no wait at all. Family members at home took pictures which were promptly received by the ship and enlarged.

"The news may not be too good, but at least we know now what to expect," one fellow passenger reflected.

A year or so later, our group had a reunion which took place at one of those beach houses, now restored. I won't call it a cottage, because it had eight bedrooms and eight baths. As I said, southern families can be large.

We ourselves took advantage of the southern Appalachians by buying a house in the mountains where cool breezes blew in summer. Not only was it a super spot for our children to come on vacation, it also gave us a chance to reciprocate for all those beach weekends with South Carolina friends. Laurel, flame azaleas and miles of rhododendron were good bait for hikers. Better yet were the mountain streams beckoning to our whitewater canoe.

"I think we should bring the canoe down to Columbia and paddle rivers in the lowlands," I proposed. "Wouldn't it be lovely, gliding through those mossy oaks, even into a swamp or two?"

I had heard that some cypress trees there were a thousand years old!

Back in Columbia I mentioned this to a University of South Carolina faculty member who had experience boating from the fall line to the sea.

"It can be exciting," he told me, "especially when snakes such as water moccasins try to climb into your canoe and you have to beat them off with your paddle. Sometimes they even drop from the trees."

Our canoe stayed in the mountains.

Some of my most vivid southern memories surround a musical treat called the "Spoleto Festival." Two weeks of culture in charming Charleston, with world-class musicians, actors and artists, was initiated while we lived in South Carolina. It continued through all our years there.

Together with two other couples—Byrnes and Mannings—we rented a cottage on Sullivan's Island near Charleston for ten days in 1976. It was such a success we kept repeating it for the next eighteen years!

As if six of us weren't enough, each family brought a dog, plus occasional children and, eventually, grandchildren. A path through sand dunes led to the beach and, a quarter-mile walk away lay an enticing revolutionary fort. In addition, sail boats, submarines and shrimpers cruised by as they emerged from Charleston harbor. It was paradise, and only twenty minutes' drive (albeit across a heart-stopping bridge) to a world of music and entertainment.

"Restaurants are going to be crammed," we wives concluded the first year. "How about taking turns on food duty, each family being responsible for a whole day's meals and then taking two days off?"

Genius, I call it. Delicacies like French toast for breakfast, intriguing sandwiches for lunch and seafood straight from fishing boats for dinner graced our days. How often in your lifetime can you be on the beach until it's time to dress for dinner, then to be greeted by such fare? Husbands helped shell shrimp and were terrific dishwashers, also very handy with the vacuum cleaner.

The music didn't always get the same raves as the food. Operas, particularly, were inclined to have wildly adventurous productions. In one of them, named *Lady Macbeth of the Matinsk District,* the main prop was a large refrigerator. The opera ended with a blinding flash representing an atom bomb, accompanied by a noise that nearly knocked us off our seats.

"One more like that and I refuse to see anything but Gilbert and Sullivan," grumbled Bernard Manning. He wouldn't have been alone, either.

I can't close this chapter without mention of Trinity Housing. In the mid-1980s homelessness was becoming a serious problem and our church decided to do its part to help. Steb was a leader on the board of directors and I was given the job of treasurer. Enough funds were rounded up to acquire a duplex, where two families (consisting of mothers and children) moved in.

It didn't take long to find out how tough life can be for single mothers with little education. Since I was in the employment business I undertook to introduce them to the office world. Both moms were smart and willing. Gradually I managed to get them into decent adult education courses using office machines and to convince an insurance company and a bank that the women would make good interns (unpaid, of course.)

They never looked back. I remember well how Tahira, when she first came, was unable to look up when talking with someone, just down into her lap. A few months into her new job and she was sitting up straight and appearing far more confident. And after she and her children left Trinity Housing I got a phone call from Florida, where she had landed a position with Disney World. I won't pretend such success stories came often, but it was heartening when they did.

Not long after, a bank had foreclosed on as 35-unit townhouse complex owned by a slum landlord, and talked our group into trying to take it over. It fell to the lot of our Housing Administrator, also a volunteer, and myself to write a Grant Application to the National Office of Housing and Development (HUD). She and I went to a national workshop on housing and found the whole country seemed to have the same idea—a discouraging discovery considering the small amount of HUD money available.

The Administrator did the background, history and layout of our project and my assignment was to spell out our proposed program along with a detailed budget.

Steb had been working with the families too.

"You've got to decide exactly what homeless families need in order to get back on their feet," he volunteered. "What have we found out so far?"

"A roof over their heads isn't enough," I contributed. "They need to find a way to survive over the long term."

"The kids need skills to help them in school, and the parents need to learn how to keep a job," he continued.

"And, maybe most important of all," I went on, "they need to find out ways to deal with real life. How to be good parents, how to handle money—frankly, just how to cope."

That became our program. We called it "Job Skills, School Skills and Life Skills" in the application, and laid out a plan and a budget to help families achieve those goals in the two years we would house them.

Lo and behold, HUD assigned us $750,000. Trinity Housing bought the property, church members pounded nails, plastered and painted, and thirty families moved in. Steb and I continued to be mentors, homework helpers and, inevitably, fundraisers for the rest of our years in Columbia, very rewarding indeed.

Nearly twenty years later I went back and it was still going strong— another enduring memory of a place we fondly called home for more than two decades.

STAGGERING VACATIONS

"Look what I found!" Steb proclaimed triumphantly one spring day in 1978. "It's a book written by a Yale professor who likes to hike. He calls it *Hut Hopping in the Austrian Alps.*

"What on earth does that mean?" I wanted to know.

"In the Alps hikers can't just camp where they want, especially above the tree line," came the explanation. "Scenery up there is fantastic, though, and the mountains extend hundreds of miles. The European solution is to build hostels—which they call huts—a day's walk apart. That way hikers can sleep and eat but not destroy the terrain. Smart, huh?"

"I'm sure it is," I agreed. "But what does that have to do with us?"

"Just think what a great vacation you and I could have! We could go this summer."

Frankly, I thought it was the worst idea for a vacation I could imagine. Still, when I recalled all the cathedrals and museums I had dragged him through, I felt a small pang of conscience.

True, we had done plenty of hiking in the past but that was mostly weekends, along with a few backpacking ventures. Nothing like this.

"Remember Nepal?" he went on. "That was the most wonderful adventure we ever had!"

An adventure it certainly had been, as readers may recall from an earlier chapter ("How to Board a Plane Through the Food Chute") but that time porters had toted our baggage, tents, and food, while Sherpas led the way, leaving us with no tough decisions whatever.

"Won't we get lost?" I asked. My own sense of direction was zero, and Steb always had to make sure we were on the right course. He also made a point of keeping me within eyesight.

"No way. The trails are all carefully laid out in this little book. It also includes stopping places for food and drink, plus sleeping accommodations. Should be easy."

So, as you may have guessed, there we were in Austria that summer. The recommended "hut hopping" vacation was divided into three sections. The first was at an altitude of 4,000-5,000 feet, the second 6,000-7,000 and the last 8,000-9,500. We had better be in good shape by that time.

So there we were in Austria. I was happy to note we could leap the first four thousand feet in one bound—by riding to the nearest hut in a cable car. Dinner there was good, but we had a shock on hearing a description of the sleeping accommodation.

"Twelve of us in one room?" we asked. "Isn't there a private bedroom somewhere?"

Our host laughed. "You won't see any private rooms up here at the top of the world," he forecast. "You're lucky tonight that you can actually have your own bunks."

That sounded ominous. Still, as explorers, Steb and I were determined to be intrepid. We duly undressed and dressed inside our sleeping bags along with the other males and females of our bunkroom.

The two of us were the last ones to start on the trail the next morning, but weren't concerned since the guidebook said it was only eight miles to the next hut. That would have been fine if the miles were level. But as we reached the top of the first height, we saw before us a huge slab-sided bowl with a tiny cleft high on the far side. So much for having a level walk. Undeterred, we picked our way slowly down the rough trail, astounded at the extraordinary rock formations around us.

So far, so good, but black clouds appeared and hidden inside them was a deluge. Feeling quite smug at having what we thought was the perfect gear—L.L.Bean ponchos—we waited for the storm to pass on. It didn't.

Trudging through the bowl and working our way up the other side took hours and our footing got more and more slippery. Sitting for a rest on a couple of rocks and peering out of our ponchos to see nothing but liquid air, we felt alone in the universe.

Finally one of us dared to voice the unmentionable.

"Do you think we've tackled more than we can handle?" Steb or I ventured.

"It's not too late in the day to turn back, but we have to do it now," the other answered on a realistic note.

Like most who can't make up their minds, we compromised.

"We'll keep on for another ten minutes, then give up," was the agreement.

To our astonishment, ten minutes later we had reached the pass, which had been invisible along with the rest of the world. Yet more surprising was the gentle, grassy slope on the other side. It was as if the bowl we had just struggled across was a meteor crater, having no relationship to the surrounding terrain. Even the rain seemed to lighten. By the time we reached our next hut, close to dinnertime, Steb was whistling and, if I had ever managed learn how, I would have too.

Sleeping accommodations were even more basic than the night before. Instead of individual bunks, a slightly-raised shelf, about seven feet in width, stretched along an entire inside wall of the building. They called it what sounded like a "matratsenlager" but if that first couple of syllables was meant to translate into "mattress," forget it. There was not the slightest sign of padding. Packs and sleeping bags had already been plunked along its length by hikers who had arrived earlier, but eventually we found room for our gear.

"Let's hope whoever built this thing used soft wood," mused Steb.

The amazing part was that when bedtime came it seemed that all those hikers not only slept soundly, but they were too exhausted even to snore. When I did waken occasionally during our three weeks in the heights I hardly heard a sound.

July was the month we were in Austria and the huts were well-filled. My problem was that the people filling them were speaking German. It was a jolt when I discovered Steb conversing with them.

"Wherever did you learn German?" I demanded, feeling a little left out.

"When I was growing up in Argentina, my parents had a German couple for their driver and cook. Since I hung around the kitchen a lot, where the cookies were, I got fairly fluent," he explained. "I haven't spoken it in years but it's strange how quickly those words come back."

I was glad for him, I guess, but I wasn't a fast enough learner to pick it up in three months, let alone three short weeks. Failing that, I tried a "Kaatzenjammer" mixture from an old comic strip.

"Schleppen zee vell?" I asked someone one morning. In return I got a hostile stare.

"Why didn't she respond?" I inquired of Steb. "I just wanted to ask if she slept well, which seemed pretty harmless."

"In the first place, 'schlepp' means to lug a load, not sleep. She probably thought you wanted her to carry your pack."

So much for communication.

The days that followed brought spectacular rewards—jagged vistas, hidden valleys and one enchanting nook after another for lunch stops. Mostly we loved it. Still, sometimes we found ourselves either clinging to a chain hammered into rock as we teetered along a skinny ledge, or threading a pass—afraid to go forward and equally afraid to go back.

"We should write a sequel called *Hut Hopping for the Weak and the Timid*" observed Steb. "The only trouble is we would have to skip too many of the best places."

Actually, we did get a little braver and certainly into better condition. The second week found us a couple of thousand feet higher but, strangely, in mountains more fully occupied than those below. Once we even found a cheese-making farm in an Alpine pasture. We were offered some of their produce and decided cheese could never taste so good again.

That night we shared a bunkroom with a woman and her two daughters. They spoke English and we had a pleasant conversation before dropping off to sleep. Then they coughed and hacked all night, admitting the next morning that they had been struggling with colds and flu. Sure enough, a few days later so did we.

"They should have quarantined themselves, the bums," Steb and I complained, but realized that, once on the trail, there wasn't much chance to do that. Luckily, we developed our own symptoms just as we reached a hut with—miracle of miracles—a private bedroom. There we snuggled into our beds and spent three delightful days recovering.

"I had no idea what a room to ourselves would do for our morale," I glowed. "It's almost worth being sick!"

Steb wasn't sure he would carry it that far, but we did enjoy a few days of leisure and short walks near the hut, rewarded as always by masses of Alpine blooms and wondrous panoramas.

The last day's hike in that region led us across a sheer slope with only a foot-wide trail, a 500-foot drop and no hand-holds. Not even a blade of grass broke the expanse of what must have been a landslide a quarter-mile across. Steb was ahead, and hadn't gone more than a hundred feet out on the bare mountainside when he stopped.

"I hate to admit this, but I've suddenly developed acute acrophobia," he lamented. "I can't take another step."

"Would it help if I went first?" I asked, not too sure I could do it either.

"I'm beginning to panic," he admitted. "We need to get off this thing *fast*."

We carefully turned around but he was too shaky even to walk back. I remembered Nepal, where I had felt the same way a few times.

"Nothing to do but go down on hands and knees," said I, the voice of experience.

So we accepted the embarrassment of heading back on all fours. Fortunately no other hikers were on hand to witness.

When we got back to the hut we abjectly confided our problem to the hut-master.

"That happens to plenty of people," he reassured us. "It's a bad place and when folks see that large slide stretching so far ahead it's easy to get a fright."

"Is there another way to the next hut?"

"In fact, there is. That hut is the last one in this section so it's downhill from here. There's an old road that works as a trail."

Immensely relieved, we appreciated a walk below tree line for a change, cherishing the thick forest surrounding us. When we reached our destination we were so close to civilization we found more of a hotel than a hut. There was even a bar.

Dining at a table for ten, the conversation was spirited. A European man next to us, when he found out we were Americans, couldn't have been more pleased.

"I was a prisoner of war in World War II," he told us delightedly. "Arizona is where I was taken. It was wonderful!"

That was hardly what we expected, but it was nice to find someone abroad who still liked Americans.

"The United States is so big they knew we couldn't escape," our new acquaintance recalled, "so we had a lot of freedom. I got a job picking cotton for a farmer and earned fifty cents a day. That meant I could buy cigarettes and candy and was pretty popular. A lot of us hadn't been happy when Adolph Hitler had forced us to go to war anyway. I had a great time in Arizona."

We and our tablemates agreed his was an unexpectedly happy war story. We were almost sorry we hadn't time to accept his invitation to visit him in Germany.

The last week of our vacation (yes, I confess I was converted to calling it that) was in glacial territory near the Italian border. Hiking was completely different when there were snowfields to cross. One day we came upon a hill and valley full of skiers—an unexpected vision.

"How did they get way up here?" we demanded of the first person who came near.

"There's a series of cable lifts on the other side of that ridge," we were told. "This is the most popular place in the area on a hot summer day."

It really was a beautiful temperature, letting us walk without jackets even at an altitude of 9,000 feet. We stayed well away from the skiers though. No sense getting plowed into this close to the end of our journey.

That last week was glorious. Glaciers around us had ends that piled up like toppling skyscrapers. Lakes below them could be jade green or blue as turquoise, and sparkled brilliantly. Every little valley was an undiscovered treasure we could never forget.

"I have to admit it," I confessed to Steb. "Your crazy idea has turned into a wonderful experience."

LONG – DISTANCE GRANDPARENTS

"This is terrible," Steb and I agreed. "Finally we have grandchildren, but all three are 900 miles away. What good is that?"

We had secretly complained for years, that, with four children ourselves, we were woefully lacking in grandchildren. Neither Jim nor Anne had married, while Peter and Allan, who had, were painfully slow about contributing to another generation.

When Katie was finally born to Caron and Peter I was nearly sixty and Steb well over that number. Naturally we were very happy, despite our age difference. Then when Nic arrived to Cathi and Allan a couple of years later, and Ian became Katie's brother a year after that, we were ecstatic.

At first, a summer house we had bought in the mountains of North Carolina became vacation headquarters for all children and grands, a highly satisfactory arrangement. The time came quickly, though, when the 16-hour drive became a chore for the parents. That was solved by our renting a big farmhouse in the Berkshire Mountains of western Massachusetts, not too far from the children's homes in Connecticut.

But were Steb and I satisfied? No.

"We need to see the grandkids more," we determined. But how?

A newspaper article came to our rescue.

"Get this," I declared one day. "It's a column called Long-Distance Grandparenting. "

"Don't be deterreds by miles," it claims. "Airlines let children fly alone starting at age seven. Why not have them visit you for a school vacation?"

That sounded good, and a couple of paragraphs later came a really terrific idea.

"When grandchildren get to be adolescents, it's safe to expect they will seem different ('obnoxious' was the word they used, though of course that would never apply to ours.) Just before that, say at age twelve, take them on a special trip. It will produce a memory they won't forget."

Steb, a born travel planner, immediately turned into an idea factory. In no time he had a list of at least fifty places we could go. After all, Katie would be seven in one more year.

We couldn't get too expansive at the beginning though. Her parents thought Columbia itself would be plenty for her first spring vacation away from home. Okay, we found entertainment right there in town. A big winner was Show-Biz Pizza—which sounded like dinner theater for the sophisticated primary school set. Sophisticated it was not, but Katie was completely smitten by mechanical gorillas and giraffes stomping around the stage while we ate pizzas in the same shapes. After dessert kids could go into a room filled with pink rubber balls. Steb and I thought we had lost her forever, but she emerged eventually with a couple of pals she had found somewhere inside the pile.

Another hit was "bumper bowling." The bowling alley, alleys and pins were normal, but gutters were filled with fat air-bumpers. Thus, once youngsters started a ball down the alley, it bounced back and forth until finally it hit some of the pins. I figured my own score was bound to improve under this system, but adults weren't allowed. Katie was enthused, especially when another youngster, age about five, wouldn't let go of his bowling ball. Thus, when he flung it as hard as he could, he slid on his stomach right down the alley along with the ball. After that they all tried it. Bodies were everywhere. A huge success.

The next vacation I ended up taking not one, but TWO trips to Disney World, since the grandchildren, though all in Connecticut schools, still had different spring weeks off. Unreasonable, I thought, but it was a blessing after all. Steb was conveniently (for him) in Europe on a University business trip. Without three arms, I wouldn't have stood a chance, dealing with all of them at once.

Nic was first. After an extremely unnerving trip to "Thunder Mountain" (actually a roller coaster ride with a Wild West motif which I might have enjoyed had I been less terrorized,) Nic found a frontier fort with guns available for shooting out every aperture. It was full of youngsters who, like my grandson, discovered they could get in their sights the people riding on the very roller coaster we had just staggered off. Seemed pretty bloodthirsty to me, but it kept them entertained for hours.

It was an intensive three days, filled with jungle river rides during which snapping crocodile jaws barely missed us; Calamity Canyon, with both an avalanche and a sudden flood; a mysterious underground journey through ghostly caves inhabited by skeletons and accompanied by eerie noises, and so on. Another three days followed when I took Katie and Ian. The amazing thing to me was that when we had seen *absolutely everything* and I let them select one last thing to go back to, each of the three chose the same one—a guy named Michael Jackson, very popular only with grown-ups, I would have thought, doing "Moon Walk" dancing!

The next year, Steb and I took all three to an island near Charleston, South Carolina, where they were able to savor a vintage aircraft carrier, destroyer, submarine, and two Revolutionary forts. The children, of course, each needed to test every gun and cannon in sight. I'm happy to report they didn't sink a thing.

When they were 12, 10 and 9 we took them to Washington, DC for a week. Have you seen the Mint, FBI, Air & Space, and Children's Museums? We have...and that was only the first day.

It happened that Nic had had a bizarre injury, and a long needle was found in the flesh near his ankle the day before our trip was due. Undaunted, he persuaded his parents to get it cut out in a hurry.

Sight-seeing Washington on crutches had its advantages. He was tucked into a wheelchair for most trips, including the White House. His cousins and I got to go with him, which made him very popular. That may (or may not) have been worth his encounter with the needle.

Myrtle Beach was another favorite destination. By then the children had outgrown the kiddie rides in a water park near our hotel, but a racing track with bumper cars was their idea of heaven. A surprise to us grandparents was how much they enjoyed as large sculpture garden down the beach. You could tell they were getting more cultured. Loudest cheers of all, though, were for that great southern delicacy: cornmeal yummies named "hush puppies."

Inevitably, the time came when Katie turned twelve. We told her to choose any place she and her grandparents could get to, enjoy, and return home during a ten-day winter or spring vacation. Having just completed a school unit on Mayan culture, she chose the Yucatan Peninsula in Mexico. We suspected she had also heard rumors about nearby Caribbean beaches.

Soon we were surrounded by a jungle full of exotic ruined temples and towering pyramids. Unfortunately, I had fallen on ice a week before and torn the rotator cuff in my shoulder, so was in a sling and couldn't attempt to climb the steeper pyramids. Katie and Steb lost no time racing up the first big one, only to find themselves at the top with acute acrophobia. Heights didn't happen to bother me at all, but watching the two of them inch down all those narrow steps was more excruciating than my shoulder. All was well when we stuck to more manageable heights.

Katie became an authority on carvings of frightening warriors who slaughtered mysterious Mayan animals, not to mention a maiden or two. The latter, however, were supposedly happy with their role. Just don't ask me to explain.

The beaches, plus lagoons filled with gorgeous fish waiting to be snorkeled over, were much less equivocal. I could even do the lagoons with my arm in a sling, as long as I used foot flippers, so Katie and I spent hours in the water. Our first foreign grandchild trip was a definite success.

Nic came next, and announced his preference was a rain forest. The Amazon would be nice, he thought, but it was too far for his ten-day Easter vacation, so we decided on Costa Rica. Wasting not a second, we spent our first days on a steep hillside overlooking Pacific beaches. There Nic was captivated by a troop of small monkeys. Those tiny animals crawled all over both boy and hammock.

"They really seem to like our balcony and trees," was his assessment, though our large nut supply, approved by the hotel as monkey food, may have had some influence. Even more enthusiasm was kindled when large apes gathered at the very tops of the tall tropical trees. They made lots of noise, as if every evening called for a party, the food for which, naturally, was the large supply of coconuts growing near the top.

My own doubts about that particular trip centered on the small-airplane journey required to cross the tropical mountains between the beach and the central valley. Landing and taking off, as was required, from the tiniest of fields, gave me considerable doubts about its sputtering engine's ability to make it over the mountains back to the center of the country. Nic's impression, of course, was entirely different.

"Wasn't it great the way they flew low so we could get a close look at the ridges?" he beamed. Oh, to have been a carefree twelve-year-old again!

San Jose, in the central valley, boasted spectacular butterfly gardens and a zoo full of peculiar animals which one would swear were, or should have been, extinct. Then we rented a jeep and plunged over another set of mountains, with a zigzag road made even more preposterous by huge mudslides.

"Bad rainy season this year," remarked the native driver casually when we pulled off at a wide spot for a little panic control. Still, the road led us to our destination—a rainforest lodge.

"Can this be the way to our cottage?" we asked as we were shown to a wooden walkway on stilts, well above ground level. It wound through foliage of high bushes and low trees, and we shared it with vivid tropical birds. As if they weren't noisy enough, the roar of a river came through our front door and howler monkeys could occasionally be heard from treetops high above.

One day a jungle trail led us onto suspension bridges over eye-popping gorges. Then came an aerial tramway which glided through the canopies of enormous tropical trees. Other days, we trekked with knowledgeable guides and took raft trips down the river.

Nearing the end of our stay, Steb asked Nic if there was anything more he would like to do.

"Grandpa, what I really came to the rainforest to see are poison-dart frogs," was the response.

That was a challenge. I asked the lodge naturalist where we might find some. The man wasn't very helpful.

"They are around," he allowed. "But they're small and you never know just where to look."

Not much assistance there.

On our last day, Nic and I were walking a self-guided trail in the jungle not far from our cottage. It was interesting but not exactly thrilling. Then came a low exclamation.

"Grandma, I think I see one," whispered Nic.

Would you believe, there was a tiny frog about the size of a silver dollar! It was black with red dots and Nic knew exactly what we had found.

"Look, there are lots!"

"But, Nic, aren't they poisonous?"

"Grandma, don't worry. A little thing like that can't hurt people like us in boots. They aren't very dangerous anyway."

He didn't reveal how he knew.

Black and red frogs were all around us in the low ground cover. Before I could stop him, Nic managed to pick one up, and suffered no ill effects. I was careful never to mention it to his parents, however.

When Ian's turn came a year later, he also elected the rain forest, so back we flew to Costa Rica. Naturally, he wanted to see everything Nic had told him about.

....

I am writing this a number of years later. Ian is now considerably older, and the other day I asked him what he remembered about the vacation.

"Very odd animals," was his immediate response. Neither of us could bring forth the names of many beyond the coati (striped like a raccoon) and caiman (which the dictionary describes as a "crocodilian") but we could both recall furry balls and slinky reptiles in intriguing sizes and shapes.

"Wonderful toucans and parrots and orchids," he continued. "Catching a big coati in our flashlights as it climbed a tree trunk in the darkness. Incredible masses of colors in the bougainvillea vines. Jungle suspension ridges. Fantastic fresh pineapple. And—best part of the trip—catching a poison-dart frog."

DEALING WITH GRIEF

I have been told that every life contains happiness and every life holds tragedy. At the moment I can think only of tragedy. That tragedy was Jim's suicide some years ago.

He lived in Tucson, Arizona, at the time, with the rest of the family on the east coast. Steb and I were in South Carolina. Jim flew east to be with us at Christmas each year, and one year he admitted he had been having bouts of depression.

I was not a stranger to depression myself (and to anxiety, which often accompanies it) because several in my mother's family had experienced that disease, which, we heard later, has a high mortality rate. My mother went to a hospital in Minneapolis for six months when my sister and I were young, and others in her large family had had similar problems.

Anyway, Jim's depression continued. Allan, our youngest son, was working on a PhD in Clinical Psychology, and we asked him to fly to Tucson to see if there was anything the family could do to help him. Allan's report was that Jim was, indeed, very depressed, but that he had good medical coverage and, as far as Allan could discern, a good doctor.

Then the dreaded news came that he had killed himself. He was 38 years old.

Jim, always thoughtful, had left a note to the police on the seat of the car which he had driven into the desert to shoot a bullet into his head. The note asked them to get the news to the Dean of the Cathedral where Steb and I went to church so, one dreary evening at 11 p.m., the Dean phoned that he was coming over to bring us bad news. We knew at once what it was, and with the Dean still there, I phoned our other three children to fly to Tucson, either with Steb and me, or straight out by themselves.

Of course it was a miserable trip. Peter, an Episcopal Priest, flew out directly to organize Jim's funeral. It took place in a beautiful church, with a large window behind the altar showing a striking view of mountains. The church was full and we were pleased, though not surprised, at the number of street children who came to tell us how much Jim had helped them.

"He got me off the streets," many said, "and started us playing games of volleyball, which then led to going back to school. He drove the school bus and always checked our schoolwork after he picked us up," they said. Jim was a very good athlete himself, placing in state swimming championships as well as volleyball.

Others talked about Jim's kindness when a neighbor needed help: "He was the only one who kept on going to visit an old man with cancer," etc.

His friends had an open house after the funeral and folks were crammed all over the floor—so we were hearing "Jim" stories during a long evening. One of his friends told us Jim's depression was bad enough, but that even worse was a recent stream of serious anxiety attacks. When such attacks were taking up a large part of each day he simply couldn't handle them. It was very sad, but somehow inspiring too, hearing that he had, even in illness, managed to help others.

What we had not realized, when we left South Carolina so hurriedly, was that our Cathedral's Dean had announced at every service the

128

Sunday after his giving us the bad news: "I want to tell you what has happened to the Stebingers." That meant a huge outpouring of attention from warm Southerners during the ensuing weeks and months, and even the burial of Jim's ashes in the cemetery outside their historic church, along with graves of local families going back to the Revolutionary War. And to think that we were Yankees living in the South!

Even with the kindness of so many friends, Steb and I had a terrible time dealing with our own grief. Periods of sleeplessness and depression were constant. Finally our doctor said he thought possibly we could help ourselves best by helping others. So we put an ad in our local newspaper announcing a new group: "Survivors of Suicide."

Surprisingly, some twenty people showed up at the first meeting, and kept enlarging. Sometimes we would have a speaker at our gatherings, but found that it was usually better to suggest a topic for each meeting and then break into small groups for discussion. Steb and I realized that most folks needed to tell their own stories, so we divided into tiny units of three or four. I must tell you it worked wonderfully. Not only did we in the Stebinger family gradually find our way back to a normal life, but so have hundreds of others.

I am writing these words many years after those heart-breaking days, and have moved far away to New England, but those South Carolina "Survivors of Suicide" still continue to meet.

God is always near to help us through the very hard times of life, and I believe his help usually comes by way of others. If your turn for tragedy should come, remember that many others, who have gone through their own tragic crises, are here to help you.

What a wonderful world it is, where we can each help another through all the years of our lives. Especially, everyone can find the love, in sorrow and in joy, of the "Jims" in their lives.

LIFE AFTER NINETY

This last chapter is being written in Cromwell, Connecticut from a retirement community called Covenant Village.

I had certainly never expected to spend my declining years in New England. However, as much as Steb and I loved Columbia and our friends in the South, it became obvious that moving north to be near family members who had relocated there was the sensible thing to do. So we moved to Connecticut.

Now, having written down a chronological series of incidents meant to give a flavor of what my life has been, I realize I have presented a fairly light-hearted version of events. Naturally, there is more to the picture.

Worst of all, of course, was Jim's tragic death. It took years and years for Steb and me to recover. After all, children are not supposed to die before their parents, and a suicide brings more guilt for parents than a normal death. We had always been a family that experienced a lot of things together, and there was one good aspect, which was that this terrible event seemed to bring the rest of us even closer.

My brother Paul also died too young, alas, at 66.

Moving on in this rather dreary vein, it wasn't long after Steb and I were installed in our hew house in Connecticut that he too began to notice deterioration. It turned out to be a fast-moving variation of Parkinson's Disease. We struggled along for a few years, but in 2001 realized a retirement community would be best for us. In 2003, Steb succumbed to his disease at 86, having remained mentally alert and incredibly good-tempered to the end. Much as I miss him, I can look back on a wonderful 58 years together.

What is it like, living in a retirement place by myself? Luckily, I enjoy it. Peter, Allan and their lovely wives live nearby. Anne, always a sweetheart, comes for a weekend about once a month, and grandchildren Kate, Nicolas and Ian are now all out of college and all fabulous.

Visits to and from my much-loved sister Adele and sister-in-law Peg occupy a pleasant share of my schedule, Adele and I having spent the month of March for the past ten years in Arizona, where many delightful cousins gather.

To my surprise, old age is a good time of life. For one thing, it's freeing. There's nothing more to prove, no more goals to set, and no more feeling that I need to please everybody. My only aim is to be useful in whatever way I can, and such opportunities appear constantly in a "continuing care" community such as mine. In theory, a lifetime of experience should bring wisdom, but often I question that, since I still do dumb things. Better just to enjoy each day, appreciating the people and events that come my way.

I happen to be lucky in the health department, for which I credit my local athletic club. I spend an hour there three times a week, using a whole batch of machines. I am still involved in various projects to help those at Covenant Village of Cromwell, where I live, and I attend plenty of symphonies, plays, even operas. I also sing in our Village Choral Group, act as one of the editors of our monthly "Village Views," belong to both reading and writing groups, and am involved in various other projects that come along. After Steb's death, I was involved for several years, taking on such roles as President of the Cromwell Covenant Village Council and even as a member of the national board of the company, with its fifteen Covenant Villages throughout the United States.

Hiking is still a favorite hobby, and there is a lovely forest with a hiking trail nearby. Surprisingly, I never encounter anyone else on the trails, though I spend at least a couple of hours a week there. I don't mind being alone, but after some of our big storms there is a lot of trail clearing to do. In fact, when some of the big trees have crashed, I simply have to start a new trail, but usually my clipper and a very up-to-date "bow saw" can take care of the debris. I'll admit to getting lost once in a while, but have a pretty good sense of direction and always carry a cell phone, so nobody needs to worry about me. In the winter, I happily bring out my snow shoes so I don't suffer from cabin fever.

As you can tell, life is very good. I assume it will continue for a while, so will plan to write another chapter at 95. See you then!

Made in the USA
San Bernardino, CA
06 September 2013